COLLINS *rambler*

dartmoor

HARVEY

The Ramblers

richard sale

HarperCollins*Publishers*, 77–85 Fulham Palace Road, London W6 8JB

The HarperCollins Website address is: www.**fire**and**water**.com

05 04 03

10 9 8 7 6 5 4 3 2

First published 2000

Series Editor Richard Sale
© in this edition HarperCollins*Publishers*
© in the text Richard Sale
© in the photographs Richard Sale, apart from the following: Tom Greeves: 13, 17, 26, 33, 39, 44, 47t, 50, 52, 77, 78, 86–7, 107, 126–7, 136, 139, 151, 152, 168. Blair Scobie: 32, 40, 41, 43, 45, 51, 55, 56, 57, 58, 62, 71, 74, 91, 99, 103, 106, 121, 125, 162. Elisabeth Stanbrook 16, 25, 28–9, 34, 35, 47b, 53, 68, 69, 80–81, 84, 94, 117, 119, 120, 128, 131, 132, 144, 159, 161
© in the maps Harvey Map Services Ltd., Doune, Perthshire
Walk profiles by Carte Blanche

We are grateful to the following members of the Ramblers' Association who kindly assisted in checking the walks in this book: Geoffrey Adams, Paul Baker, C D Blake, Mr & Mrs A R Bradford, Roy Delbridge, P E Dodd, Matthew Johnson, Sue Langford, Ron Lovell, Ralph Morgan, Rodney Smith and Dr A E Walton. Special thanks are due to Ronald Bagshaw for his sound advice on the routes and maps.

The profiles given for each walk give an indication of the steepness and number of climbs on the route. The times on the profiles are calculated according to the Naismith formula which suggests one hour for each five map kilometres (three map miles) covered, together with an additional 30 minutes for each 300m (1,000ft) of ascent. For most walkers the formula underestimates the time taken for several reasons. Firstly few walkers complete a walk as a route march; secondly, there is no allowance for the terrain crossed, and it is easier to walk quickly over short grass than rough moor; thirdly, there is no allowance for stopping to admire the view, places of interest etc; and finally there is no allowance for rest stops. Rest stops tend to become both longer and more frequent as the walk length increases, so the time error increases as walks get longer. Please check yourself against the times on the first walks you attempt to gauge the time you will take on others.

ISBN 0 00 220166 6

Designed and produced by Drum Enterprises Ltd.
Printed and bound in Great Britain by Scotprint

CONTENTS

How to use this book

This book contains route maps and descriptions for 30 walks. Each walk is graded (see p.3) and areas of interest are indicated by symbols (see below). For each walk particular points of interest are denoted by a capital letter both in the text and on the map (where the letter appears in a red box). In the text the route descriptions are prefixed by lower-case letters. We recommend that you read the whole description, including the tinted box at the start of each walk, before setting out.

Key to maps

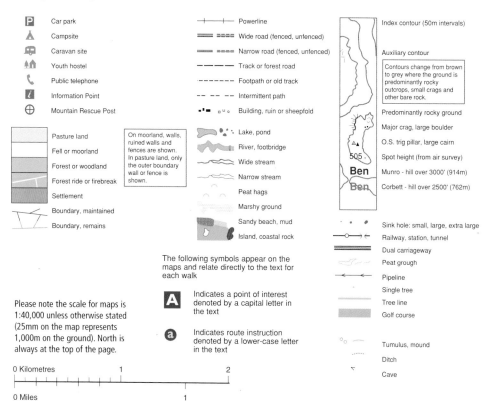

P Car park

Å Campsite

⚏ Caravan site

⚏ Youth hostel

☎ Public telephone

i Information Point

⊕ Mountain Rescue Post

Pasture land

Fell or moorland

Forest or woodland

Forest ride or firebreak

Settlement

Boundary, maintained

Boundary, remains

On moorland, walls, ruined walls and fences are shown. In pasture land, only the outer boundary wall or fence is shown.

——+—— Powerline

===== ==== Wide road (fenced, unfenced)

===== ==== Narrow road (fenced, unfenced)

— — — — Track or forest road

- - - - - - Footpath or old track

-- -- -- Intermittent path

▪▪■ ▫ᵘ◦ Building, ruin or sheepfold

Lake, pond

River, footbridge

Wide stream

Narrow stream

Peat hags

Marshy ground

Sandy beach, mud

Island, coastal rock

The following symbols appear on the maps and relate directly to the text for each walk

A Indicates a point of interest denoted by a capital letter in the text

a Indicates route instruction denoted by a lower-case letter in the text

Index contour (50m intervals)

Auxiliary contour

Contours change from brown to grey where the ground is predominantly rocky outcrops, small crags and other bare rock.

Predominantly rocky ground

Major crag, large boulder

O.S. trig pillar, large cairn

505 · Spot height (from air survey)

Ben Munro - hill over 3000' (914m)

Ben Corbett - hill over 2500' (762m)

· · ● Sink hole: small, large, extra large

—○—← Railway, station, tunnel

Dual carriageway

Peat grough

←—←— Pipeline

Single tree

Tree line

Golf course

Tumulus, mound

Ditch

Cave

Please note the scale for maps is 1:40,000 unless otherwise stated (25mm on the map represents 1,000m on the ground). North is always at the top of the page.

0 Kilometres   1   2

0 Miles   1

Key to symbols

The walks in this book are graded from 1–5 according to the level of difficulty, with 1 being the easiest and 5 the most difficult. We recommend that walks graded 4 or higher (or grade 3 where indicated) should only be undertaken by experienced walkers who are competent in the use of map and compass and who are aware of the difficulties of the terrain they will encounter. The use of detailed maps is recommended for all routes.

At the start of each walk there is a series of symbols that indicate particular areas of interest associated with the route.

 Birdlife

 Good views

 Other wildlife

 Historical interest

 Wild flowers

 Woodland

INTRODUCTION

Southern England is not noted for its wildernesses. To the lover of the outdoors the north of England, with north Wales and Scotland are the lands of opportunities. To the south of the Peak there is only low land, a country where the walking is contained to farmland and the coast. Too often Dartmoor is dismissed as just another part of this 'soft' country. But those that are inclined to be so dismissive are wrong: rising to the highest peak in Southern England – High Willhays is usually described as the highest point in England south of Kinder Scout, but there is actually higher ground on the Herefordshire side of the eastern Black Mountains ridge on the Welsh border – and extending to hundreds of square miles of beautiful, but uncompromising moorland, Dartmoor is a wonderful wilderness, as exciting in its way as any of Britain's uplands.

Around 300 million years ago the curiously, but exquisitely, named Variscan Orogeny (an example of a geological squeezing caused by plate tectonics) created the Cornubian Mountains along the length of what is now Britain's South West Peninsula. Into the roots of these mountains poured volcanic magma. When the softer, overlying mountains had eroded away this magma formed a series of six granite masses which characterise the Peninsula: Dartmoor lies in Devon; the other masses forming Bodmin and Penwith Moors, Hensbarrow and Carnmenellis in Cornwall; and the Scilly Isles. Of these Dartmoor is the largest. The granite forms the basis of the Dartmoor National Park, which covers over 350 sq. miles (over 900 sq. km), which was created in October 1951. The National Park was set up to preserve Dartmoor's rugged landscape which, though it has a circling border of pleasant villages, is as uninhabited as the mountain parks of England and Wales.

The geologist recognises several forms of granite on Dartmoor, the forms being dependent on how fast the molten magma cooled to form the rock. The fastest cooling creates a coarse-grained rock with deep fissures which weathering turns into the fantastic tors that are such a marvellous feature of Dartmoor. It is an irony that only the existence of an easy-to-reach, finer-grained rock saved the tors for today's walker. Had the fine-grained rock not been so easily quarried, the 18th century quarrymen would have destroyed the tors long before they became a target for those with the leisure time to seek them out.

All of Dartmoor's granite types form a thin, acidic soil which supports a limited range of plants and encourages the formation of peat and peat bogs. These bogs define the moor in popular imagination. In 1586 William Camden wrote of 'squalida montana Dartmore' and, more recently, Sabine Baring Gould, in his *Book of Dartmoor* published in 1900, recorded the view of a Plymouth tailor – 'I solemnly swear to you, Sir, nothing will ever induce me to set foot on Dartmoor again. If I chance to see it from the Hoe, Sir, I'll avert my eyes. How can people think to come here for pleasure – for pleasure, Sir! ... only unwholesome-minded individuals can love Dartmoor'. When Conan Doyle set *The Hound of the Baskervilles* on Dartmoor, with, as its centrepieces, the fearsome Grimpen Mire (almost certainly modelled on Foxtor Mires), Dartmoor's reputation as a place of leg-devouring bogs of interest only to fools was established.

It would be foolish to suggest that Dartmoor does not deserve, in part at least, its reputation. The bogs can, indeed, be fierce. But they have an undoubted beauty too, and are separated by areas of drier moor. The high central dome of the moor, where the major bogs lie, is also surrounded by more fertile land where there are areas of upland heath, grass moor and magnificent wooded valleys. And even the central dome has areas of surprise. As an example, just a short distance north of Two Bridges is Wistman's Wood, a remnant patch of oak woodland, the trees bent and gnarled by winter's strong, cold winds. On a misty morning the twisted trees are a magical sight. The wood is also home to rare mosses and lichens.

Wistman's Wood is an excellent example to choose when considering Dartmoor. For all its apparent limitations as a habitat for wildlife Dartmoor is, in fact, a remarkable oasis for some very rare species. The Dartford warbler has become a resident as the climate has improved over the last few years, and the woodlark and cirl bunting are relatively common here though rare elsewhere. Dartmoor is the last stronghold of the high brown and marsh fritillary butterflies, and the white admiral has recently recolonised the moor. The southern damselfly thrives here, but is internationally threatened, and Dartmoor is one of the few British places where the keeled-skimmer dragonfly breeds. The blue ground

Goldsmith's Cross and Fox Tor mines

beetle is found nowhere else in Britain. Of plants, the delicate, white Irish lady's tresses and the equally delicate, but yellow, flax-leaved St John's wort are found nowhere else in England and Wales. The world population of one species of lichen, *Graphina pauciloculata*, is found in only two places on Dartmoor and one on nearby Bodmin Moor. The walker may not see any of these species of course – but is likely to see a buzzard working the thermals off the moorland edge or hear the rippling call of the curlew.

Wistman's Wood is also a good example because of its place in Dartmoor mythology as it was to the wood that locals believed the Devil chased the souls of the dead. Dartmoor is a land of legends, most of them dark and all of them adding an extra ·dimension to a walk. The legends grew from the landscape, for not only is the moor a brooding place when night or the mist falls, but it also has a number of ancient sites – standing stones, stone rows, burial mounds – that add their own evocative presence.

The Walks

The walks have been chosen to explore all aspects of Dartmoor – its scenery, natural history, ancient and mythical places and its more recent history: the moor of the miners and quarrymen.

The B3212 and B3357, which meet at Two Bridges, divide the moor into four very uneven sections. To the north is the highest land, while to the south is the most featureless moor, a real wilderness. Within the book the outlying sections of the National Park, those west of the A386 and east of the A382 are included in the northern moor. The smaller areas of moor created by the crossing roads lie to the east and west. To the west is a small triangle that includes the best of the moor's prehistoric sites and a legendary tor; to the east is Widecombe, the most famous moorland village, and Haytor, the most popular of the tors.

These four moorland areas are explored by a series of circular walks. Most of the routes follow defined tracks or paths. Much of Dartmoor is an open access area, that is the public has the right to roam freely so detours and short cuts can be easily organised. Nevertheless, for the sake of defining a walk, tracks and landmarks must be included.

Rock basin, Kes Tor

In addition to the moorland walks, three walks on the South Devon coast are given. It is sometimes possible to stand on the southern edge of Dartmoor and to view a sun-drenched coast from within a shroud of dark cloud/mist. On those days many walkers are tempted to desert the moor – if only temporarily – to enjoy the delights of one of the finest stretches of coastline in Britain.

For each walk an approximate time is given. These are based on the well-known 'Naismith Formula' which allows one hour for each 5 map-km (3 map-miles) plus an extra half-hour for each 300m (1,000ft) of ascent. These strictures have been modified to allow for the terrain covered by each walk: it is quicker to travel a few hundred metres along a surfaced track than across the moorland of north Dartmoor. It also takes less energy and here the major problem with Naismith is revealed. The formula assumes an unladened walker of limitless energy who wastes no time admiring the view. Real walkers, as opposed to Naismith automatons, take rests (which are both more frequent and last longer as they become tired) and stop for the view, or the wildlife, or any of another dozen or more reasons. Please use the times as a guide only, modifying them according to your personal characteristics after completing a couple of routes.

The walks are ordered by geographical area: they start in the north and move south, and within each of the four areas the walks are ordered by completion time. Each of the walks is graded in terms of difficulty on a rating of 1–5; 1 being the easiest and 5 the most difficult.

The Dartmoor Firing Ranges

The Ministry of Defence has a large training area on the northern moor which includes three live firing ranges. Live firing takes place on a number of days each year, but at other times the public has access to the ranges in exactly the same way that access is granted to the moor's other public access areas.

The ranges are called Okehampton, Merrivale and Willsworthy. On the ground the ranges are indicated by Range Posts in red and white, and by Range Notice Boards on the main approaches which give range information. When the ranges are in use red flags are flown from flagpoles erected on certain high points. If the firing is at night these show red lights. When the flags or lights are showing, entry into the ranges is forbidden. (It is also, of course, extremely dangerous.) In addition to live firing, so-called dry training also takes place within the ranges. This involves pyrotechnics and blank ammunition which sound like live firing but are not. Access is permitted when such dry training is in progress.

When you are walking within the ranges do not pick up or disturb any metal objects. Such actions are potentially dangerous and are an offence under MoD Range Bylaws. Any object discovered should be reported to the police or the Camp Commandant of Okehampton Camp.

Please note that the ranges adjoin one other. If, therefore, there is firing on two or more ranges simultaneously there is no safe corridor between the ranges.

Information on Firing Times can be obtained in advance. You can avoid red flags spoiling your trip by reading local newspapers on Fridays, or check the notice boards in local police stations. The National Park Information offices, many Tourist Information Centres, post offices within the National Park, and some pubs also display the times.

There is also a telephone answering service on the following numbers:

Exeter 01392 270164
Okehampton 01837 52939
Paignton 01803 559782
Plymouth 01752 501478

Firing may be cancelled at short notice even after the publication of firing notices. If the red flags are not flying by 09.00 from April to September inclusive and by 10.00 from October to March inclusive, then no live firing will take place that day. Any firing or explosions you then hear will be blank cartridges or fireworks.

Transport

Being largely uninhabited, Dartmoor suffers from a lack of public transport. Buses do follow the roads that bisect the moor, and also visit most of the villages. But these buses are infrequent and the walker will occasionally need to modify a walk or extend it to make use of them.

At the moor's edge the situation is better, particularly at the southern edge where relatively frequent services follow the A38 between Exeter and Plymouth. The South Devon coast is also well serviced by buses. The start of one or two walks in the south are also reached by trains.

Information on the available services are given for each walk. A booklet on the public transport options on Dartmoor (buses and trains) is published annually and can be obtained from the moor's Tourist Information Centres (at Haytor, Newbridge, Postbridge, and Princetown: there are also TICs just off the moor at Ivybridge, Okehampton and Tavistock) or by telephoning Exeter (01392) 382800. The same number can also be used to obtain bus timetables for the coast.

Weather
A weather forecast for the moor (as well as Exmoor and the remainder of the South-west Peninsula) is available by ringing 0891 141203. The forecast covers the next 48–72 hours and is updated daily at 7am and 7pm.

Warning sign at the boundary of the National Park

LYDFORD GORGE

MAPS:
OS Landranger Sheets 191 or 201, OS Outdoor Leisure Sheet 28

START/FINISH:
There are National Trust car parks at both ends of the gorge, at 501832 and 509844. The latter is near Lydford Bridge, close to Lydford village where there is also a car park (510848). Lydford is on the route of several DevonBuses

DISTANCE/ASCENT:
3½ miles (5.5km)/330ft (100m)

APPROXIMATE TIME:
2–3 hours

HIGHEST POINT:
Lydford village 755ft (230m)

REFRESHMENTS:
There is an inn/hotel in the village and a NT cafe near the car park at the northern end of the gorge

ADVICE:
A straightforward, well-signed walk, chiefly on constructed paths. The damp, shady sections of the gorge are usually slippery. The gorge is only open from its southern (waterfall) end from November to March

Please note that the gorge is only open from April to November from 10am to 5.30pm

Tthis is the only walk in the book for which the walker will pay for the privilege of completion. That might sound a good reason for avoiding the route, but the temptation to go elsewhere should be avoided: Lydford Gorge is a magnificent walk, tree-lined, and a complete contrast to the wild moorland for which Dartmoor is famous.

A   Lydford
In 577AD the Saxons defeated the Britons (the Celts) at the battle of Dyrham near Bristol. The Saxon victory split the Britons in two, pushing them into Wales and the South-west Peninsula. On the peninsula the Saxons continued their advance, forcing the Britons to retreat into what is now Cornwall. The Saxons dug Offa's Dyke between themselves and the Britons of Wales, but they had no such structure along the Devon/Cornwall border. As a result, during the Viking raids of the early 9th century the Danes attacked not only by sailing their longships along the Thames and the south coast, but along the Tamar, allowing them to strike east towards Wessex. The raiders were beaten back, though King Alfred was forced to retreat to Somerset before finally putting the invaders to flight. In the years of relative peace which followed Alfred built a series of 'burhs', fortresses, to defend Wessex against a renewed onslaught. On the western border of Wessex he placed four forts, at Exeter, Barnstaple and Totnes to protect the riverways into Devon, and at Lydford in case of a renewed attack along the Tamar.

Lydford was an ideal defensive site, the Saxon fort occupying the sharp ridge of land between the River Lyd and one of its tributary streams. The rivers formed a moat on three sides, a square of ramparts offering further protection. On the eastern side the ramparts linked the rivers, crossing the minor road (leaving the village towards the A386) near Nicholls Hall Chapel. The fortress was entered through a gate on its southern side, a track leading down to a ford of the Lyd. The Saxons called the river 'Lild' – noisy stream – the village being named for the 'Lild ford'.

Within the ramparts the Saxons laid out a grid pattern of streets which the present village still follows. The importance of the Saxon village is reflected in its having a Royal mint, its

coins – called Lydford pennies – being struck from locally mined silver. Silver Street, at the eastern end of the village, is a reminder of the Saxon mint.

Lydford Castle from St Petrock's churchyard. Site of the tinner's prison

Lydford-struck coins can be seen in the Castle Inn and in the British Museum. There are also a large number in the Royal Stockholm Museum: some of these were doubtless plunder from Viking raids, though many others were Danegeld, the bribe (raised by taxation) paid by Wessex to keep the Danes from raiding the Saxon kingdom. Despite the victories over the Danes and Alfred's ring of forts, the raiders still represented a threat: in 997 a raiding party sailed up the Tamar, then disembarked to sack and burn Lydford and Tavistock.

The Normans occupied the Saxon fortress site, building a castle against the western ramparts. But soon Lydford's

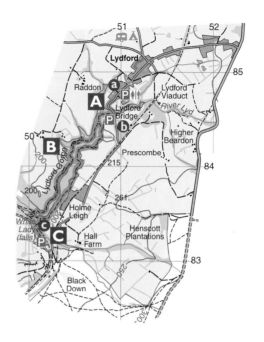

strategic importance declined, and the bigger towns of Okehampton and Tavistock became Dartmoor's major market centres. This may explain why little of the Norman Castle remains – it was probably only a wooden keep. What is now called Lydford Castle, the imposing square block beside the church, was nothing of the sort, having been erected as a 'strong building' (i.e. a prison) in the late 12th century when the village was the site of the Dartmoor Stannary Courts which dealt with those who had broken local mining laws. The prison was on two floors and a basement, its occupants being kept with little light or food, no heat or sanitation, and in constant fear of their lives. The prison had a fearsome reputation which was captured in a poem by William Browne of Tavistock:

I oft have heard of Lydford Law
How in the morn they hang and draw
and sit in judgement after
At first I wondered at it much
But soon I found the matter such
As it deserves no laughter

They have a castle on a hill
I took it for some old windmill
The vanes blown off by the weather.
Than lie therein one night 'tis guessed
'Twere better to be stoned or pressed
Or hanged, ere you come thither.

The idea of punishment before judgement is based on the curious set up of the Stannary Court. The Court of Swainmote tried and sentenced offenders, but its decision had to be ratified by the Court of Justice Seat. However, the latter had no power to overturn a conviction or sentence and as it met much less frequently than the lower court was often in the position of ratifying a sentence that had already been carried out.

The Stannary Court was immensely powerful, the power adding to the reputation of the prison. When Richard Strode the MP for Plympton complained about local mining techniques, which caused a great deal of debris to be washed down the rivers from Dartmoor, silting up Plymouth harbour and threatening the livelihood of his constituents, he was kidnapped and thrown in Lydford Castle's basement, the nastiest of its 'rooms'. Only when he agreed to stop his protests was he released. Strode could be seen as an early proponent of green issues, and his imprisonment also resulted in a law which allowed free speech on any topic within Parliament.

Beside Lydford Castle stands St Petrock's Church, named for a Celtic missionary active in Cornwall during the early 6th century. The first church on the site was probably a wooden Saxon building, the present church dating from the 13th century, though it was modified and enlarged in the 15th, the fine pinnacled tower being added at that time. Interestingly, to minimise inconvenience to the congregation during the building of the tower it was built 2ft (60cm) from the church and a linking section was added later. The tower now houses the old village stocks. Despite its never having been a large village, the stocks could 'accommodate' four offenders at a time, and could also cater for different size legs. Look, too, for the beautifully carved pew ends, dating from the 1920s, the rood screen, carved to a medieval design in the early 1900s and the reredos, erected in 1923. In the churchyard, close to the porch is the Watchmaker's Tomb, a table tomb whose famous inscription is a little difficult to read. The inscription runs:

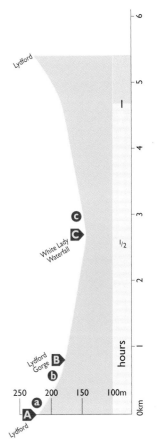

Please note: time taken calculated according to the Naismith Formula (see p.2)

The Watchmaker's Tomb in Lydford Churchyard

Here lies in a horizontal position
The outside case of
George Routleigh, Watchmaker
Whose abilities in that line were an honour
To his profession
Integrity was the mainspring
And prudence the regulator
Of all the actions of his life.
Humane, generous and liberal
His hands never stopped
Till he had relieved distress.
So nicely regulated were all his motions
That he never went wrong
Except when set agoing
By people
Who did not know
His key.
Even then he was easily
Set right again.
He had the art of disposing his time
So well
That his hours glided away
In one continual round
Of pleasure and delight
Till an unlucky minute put a period to
His existence.
He departed this life
Nov. 14. 1802
Aged 57
Wound up
In hopes of being taken in hand
By his Maker
And of being thoroughly cleaned, repaired
And set agoing
In the world to come.

a   Those starting from the Lydford village car park (510848) walk past the castle and church before descending to Lydford Bridge. Cross the bridge, from which there is a good view of the gorge, and turn right to the National Trust site. Pay the entrance fee for the gorge and head towards the river.

B   Lydford Gorge

Lydford Gorge was created when the south-flowing River Lyd was captured by another stream which sent its waters westward. The raising of the Dartmoor plateau increased the drop of the river, adding to its erosive power and the rapid carving of the gorge we see today. The extent of the erosion can be readily seen at the White Lady Waterfall where a small tributary of the Lyd falls 100ft (30m) over a cliff of hard rock to reach the excavated gorge floor. The corrosive effect of the river can also be seen at the Devil's Cauldron and Tunnel Falls. At both sites, but particularly the former, there are potholes rubbed round and smooth by swirling waters carrying boulders and pebbles. Once a pit has been dug in the river's bedrock the rapidly moving pebbles widen and deepen it, smoothing the sides in much the same way as a shot-blaster cleans and smooths corroded metal.

Lydford Gorge – leafy greenery and rushing water

The Gorge is a haven for plant and wildlife, the chief justification for the National Trust's ownership and entrance fees being the preservation of the superb landscape: though such narrow, steep-sided gorges are rarely capable of sustained agriculture free access by sheep would doubtless have a harmful affect. The River Lyd is home to brown trout, and dippers are often seen in its waters. On the banks pied and grey wagtails can usually be seen. The plant life varies from oaks in the drier sections to a superb collection of mosses and lichens in the damper areas. The Devil's Cauldron is particularly good for the latter, its walls hanging with dripping greenery. The Gorge's ferns include hart's tongue, polypody and hard fern, while the flowers include the delicate wood sorrel, the green-flowered dog's mercury, wood anemone and, in spring, primroses, bluebells and violets. The flowers attract many butterflies, including the rare purple hairstreak and silver-washed fritillary. The elephant hawk moth can also be seen occasionally.

The woodland birds include nuthatches, great spotted woodpeckers, blackcaps and spotted flycatchers. The woods are also home to a variety of small mammals, rodents, weasels and stoats, as well as larger species – badgers and the occasional red deer.

b   From the National Trust entrance, follow the path that takes a line above the river's left bank. This soon reaches a path junction at a bridge over the disused GWR line from Okehampton and Launceston to Plymouth. The Gorge's southern entrance is reached by climbing the path ahead, but the walk continues by turning right. The path soon reaches a fork. Here the 'short and steep' route to the river bears right, following an occasionally stepped path downhill. The left fork follows the 'long and easy' path to reach the same point, close to the waterfall.

C   White Lady Waterfall

An old legend claims that if someone falling over the cliff down which the waterfall drops sees the ghost of a white lady they will not drown in the river at the fall's base. But considering the drop – about 100ft (30m) – and the shallowness of the pool at the base it is unlikely that anyone would survive the fall long enough to drown. An alternative version of the tale claims that seeing the White Lady saves you from drowning if you fell into the river at this point, which seems more plausible.

c From the waterfall cross the bridge over the River Lyd and follow the path which stays close to the river's right bank. This is the finest section of the walk, with beautiful views. After about 1,200 yards (1,100m) the path goes through a short rock tunnel where the Gorge narrows. The river here runs over Tunnel Falls, a series of short waterfalls and potholes. After a further 600 yards (550m) Pixie Glen is reached, one of the most picturesque sections of the Gorge.

Just beyond the Glen there is another footbridge. Cross this for the quickest way back to the National Trust buildings. To reach the impressive Devil's Cauldron, continue along the river's right bank. The Cauldron is approached by an engineered pathway, with steps and a bridge section, all wet and slippery and requiring care. After viewing the potholes return along the path, bearing left to reach the entrance buildings.

White Lady Waterfall

THE TEIGN VALLEY

MAPS:
OS Landranger Sheet 191, OS
Outdoor Leisure Sheet 28

START/FINISH:
At 743899, Fingle Bridge. There
is roadside parking close to the
Anglers' Rest Inn, and a car
park on the other side of the
bridge. Parking is also available
on NT land at 725903

Fingle Bridge is not served by
buses, but several DevonBuses
run close to the route

DISTANCE/ASCENT:
4 miles (6.5km)/ 500ft (150m)

APPROXIMATE TIME:
2 hours

HIGHEST POINT:
About 790ft (240m) on
Drewston Common

REFRESHMENTS:
The Anglers' Rest Inn, at the
start and Castle Drogo NT

ADVICE:
A very easy walk, though care is
needed on the return (riverside)
path which can be muddy and
slippery, especially going up the
cut rock steps under the
landslip, after rain or when the
ground is icy

Just a mile or so south of East Dart Head is Teign Head, where
the North Teign River rises. A curiosity of local geography
ensures that the northernmost of the two rivers flows
south, while the southernmost flows north. To the west of
Chagford the North Teign joins the South Teign, the combined
river meandering north-eastwards through a fine pastoral
landscape until it reaches a last outlier of Dartmoor upland.
There the river is confined within the steep, tight gorge that
forms the basis of this walk.

A   Fingle Bridge

It is thought that there was a ford of the Teign at this point from
earliest times, that making it the obvious place for a bridge,
though there is no confirmed record of one before 1607.
Despite that, the style of the bridge leads historians to date it
to Elizabethan times. It was probably built for packhorses
hauling charcoal from the local oak woods and flour from Fingle
Mill which was powered by the Teign. The mill lay about 300
yards (274m) downstream of the bridge, on the right bank.
Little remains as it was destroyed by fire in 1894.

With its pointed buttresses (whose tops were recessed so that
packhorses could pass) three arches and wooded setting, the
bridge is as picturesque a river crossing as exists on
Dartmoor.

Fingle Bridge seen through early morning mist in the Teign valley

a From Fingle Bridge head north along the road towards Drewsteignton for about 150 yards (137m) to reach the signed 'Hunter's Path' on the left. Take this bridleway, climbing west through fine woodland to reach open hillside. Continue along the path to reach Sharp Tor (728899) from where there is a superb view along the tight Teign Gorge, and also of Cranbrook Down, the site of a hillfort, to the southeast across the gorge.

B Teign Gorge Hillforts

There are two Iron Age hillforts defending the Teign near Fingle Bridge, Cranbrook Castle lying above the southern bank and the larger Prestonbury Castle lying on the northern, directly above the bridge. The ditch of Cranbrook Castle encloses an area of about 7 acres (2.8ha): the fort is a marvellous viewpoint, especially east towards Cosdon Hill. Prestonbury is much larger, its ramparts enclosing about 25 acres (10.1ha). There is no evidence that they were occupied by opposing forces, but had they been, they would have been precursors of Civil War conflicts in the area. Then Chagford, to the west, was a Parliamentarian stronghold while Dunsford, to the east, was Royalist. A cross engraved on a granite block just to the south of Fingle Bridge marks the place where a Royalist soldier was killed in one skirmish. In the gorge at the other end of our walk, Sidney Godolphin, a Roundhead poet, was killed in another fight.

b From Sharp Tor, continue west along the Hunter's Path, soon reaching steps, on the right, which allow access to Castle Drogo (N.T.).

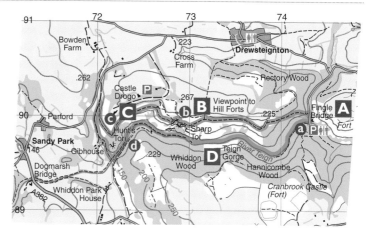

C Castle Drogo

Although requiring a detour from the walk, few will miss a visit to this remarkable building. The curious name derives from a grandson of Richard, Duke of Normandy who was granted the local area after the Norman conquest. The estate eventually passed to Richard's grandson, who was called Drew or Drogo, the two apparently being interchangeable. Drew has passed down to us in Drewsteignton, the name of the nearby village, while Drogo has given us Castle Drogo. The castle was built for Julius Drewe, founder of the Home and Colonial grocery store chain in the late 19th century. Drewe's cousin, Richard Peek, was rector of Drewsteignton and during regular visits to the village Drewe became convinced that his name meant he was a descendant of the old Norman lord.

In 1910 Drewe moved to Devon and employed Edwin Lutyens to build him a castle befitting his assumed ancestry. The original plan was for a vast castle, but the 1914–18 War imposed restrictions on materials and workmen which, together with Lutyens' better judgement, scaled the plan

Looking south towards Chagford and the north-eastern moor from near Castle Drogo

down by more than half. Even so, the angular granite castle, which took 20 years to build (though it was largely complete by 1925) is imposing. Sadly, Drewe only enjoyed his castle, and the marvellous view of Dartmoor from it, for a few years before dying in 1931, aged 75. He was buried in Torquay, his grave marked by a granite headstone designed by Lutyens. In 1974 the Drewe family gave the castle to the National Trust.

Inside, the castle is a mix of the austere – bare granite walls – and the sumptuous. Some of the furnishings reflect Drewe's enthusiasm for his supposed ancestor – though they are copies of medieval works rather than early Norman – while others are the height of early 20th century fashion. Outside, there are a series of excellent gardens, planted with roses, herbs and rhododendron, and some good shrubberies.

c   Follow the path to Hunt's Tor (722898, incorrectly named as Hunter's Tor on the OS maps). Here the path bears right (NNW) and descends to reach a signpost (at 720901). Follow the arrow sharp left for the 'Fisherman's Path', bearing left at a path junction to reach Gibhouse, a delightful thatched cottage. Just before the cottage the path goes left: take this, following it to reach an iron bridge over the Teign (722896). Do not cross: instead, bear left and north-east to follow the Teign's left bank.

D   Teign Gorge
This section of the walk is beautiful, with sunlight flicking through the trees and the water close by. The trees are mainly oak and birch, but with some beech, ash and sycamore, and alder on the river bank. All three types of British woodpecker (green, great and lesser spotted) and treecreepers can be found in the woods, while dippers, grey wagtails and kingfishers are often seen in or beside the river. There are also otters in the Teign here. The wood is home to fallow deer.

The dense shadows are not ideal for butterflies, but silver-washed fritillaries and wood whites can be seen. The shadows are equally hard on flowers, but rosebay willowherb and wood anemone thrive, and there are yellow irises by the river. More colourful, but a good deal rarer, is the poisonous fly agaric toadstool (*Amanita muscaria*).

d   The Fisherman's Path follows the river back to Fingle Bridge, offering few problems, though steps cut in the rock are used to negotiate a landslip below Sharp Tor, and the path can be slippery especially when icy.

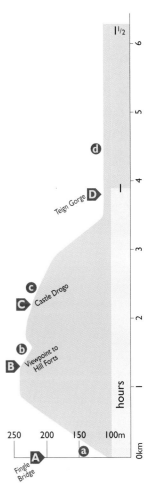

Please note: time taken calculated according to the Naismith Formula (see p.2)

TAVY CLEAVE

MAPS:
Harvey Dartmoor North, OS
Landranger Sheet 191, OS
Outdoor Leisure Sheet 28

START/FINISH:
At 537824, the car park at the
aptly named Lane End
(Lanehead OS), the end of the
minor road heading north-west
from Mary Tavy through
Horndon

Horndon (about 2½ miles (4km)
south of Lane End) is a terminus
of DevonBus 95, though the bus
runs on Fridays only

DISTANCE/ASCENT:
4 miles (6.5km), 550ft (170m);
longer route 6 miles (9.7km)

APPROXIMATE TIME:
2–3 hours

HIGHEST POINT:
Ger Tor 1,463ft (446m)

REFRESHMENTS:
None on the walk, but available
in Mary Tavy 3 miles (5km) to
the south-west

ADVICE:
Mainly easy walking, though the
rocks in Tavy Cleave can be wet
and slippery, requiring care and
dexterity. Navigation is
straightforward, but map and
compass should be carried

This walk lies within one of the
Army's Dartmoor Firing Ranges.
Please read the section on the
ranges (see pp.9–10) before
setting out

The River Tavy, draining the eastern edge of the high moor, is claimed to be the fastest river in England, and second only to Spey in Scotland's Cairngorms of British rivers, falling over 1,000ft (300m) in little more than 7 miles (11km). Perhaps not surprisingly it has cut an impressive gorge. That gorge, Tavy Cleave, is the target of this walk.

a   From the car park enter Willsworthy Range (see Advice below) and head north-east towards Ger Tor, soon reaching a leat.

A   Mine Leat
The leat supplied water to power the Wheal Friendship copper mine near Mary Tavy, its water powering a total of 17 waterwheels, ten used to pump water from the mine, the rest turning the crushing mills. Side channels also powered wheels at Wheal Jewell (the mine site now occupied by a long, thin reservoir) and Wheal Betsy. In each case the water was returned to the Wheal Friendship leat so as to provide maximum power for the larger mine.

The construction of water channels such as this leat has an impressive history stretching back at least to the Romans who were the masters at creating long channels with minimal drops to take water to their towns. Here the leat takes water from the Tavy and carefully contours it around the moor. The leat is narrow enough to be jumped, to assist maintenance men, but also occasionally bridged to allow equipment to be taken across.

b   Cross the leat by bridge or inspired leap, then continue along the path which leads uphill over Nattor Down to reach Ger Tor (547831).

B   Ger Tor
The tor is said to be named for the tin miners' slang expression for one of their trial excavations, of which there were a great number on the western side, below the peat. A possible alternative variation is from Gert Tor. It is usually assumed that 'gert' (or 'girt') means great in West Country dialects, and that was indeed the case, but it could also mean a steep sided

Winter light on a prehistoric hut circle near Ger Tor, and the Tavy Valley

valley, another form of cleave. In this case it would have to be the second version of the name, for Ger Tor could hardly have warranted the name 'great' in anybody's eyes.

From the tor there is an excellent view west into the valley of the River Tavy, and east across Tavy Cleave to Fur Tor. Standon Down, to the south, has a large number of hut circles across its summit leading some experts to talk of a complete Bronze Age 'town'. There is also evidence of a Bronze Age settlement on Ger Tor with several hut circles and a number of 'reaves', the low walls which separated cultivated fields. Further east, near the Dead Lake stream, a tributary of the Tavy, and on Watern Oke, there is more evidence of Bronze Age occupation. A walk that way is an extension of the suggested route, but offers one of the easiest climbs of Fur Tor: follow the Tavy to Sandy Ford (at 572833), close to which are the ruins of a tinner's hut, then strike east to the Tor.

c   From Ger Tor (547831) head north then north-north-east towards Hare Tor (551843), then bear right through further hut circles (550834), some of which are well preserved. Walk on to the obvious cleft directly ahead in the rocks of the Tavy Cleave Tors (HARVEY map 554834) for an even better view up

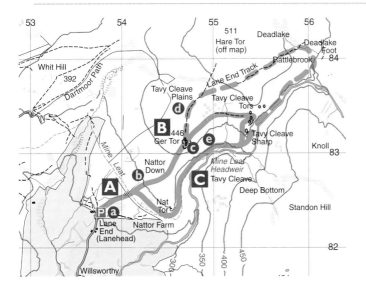

Please note: time taken calculated according to the Naismith Formula (see p.2)

the Cleave. Turn round and walk down the steepish way to the Cleave past the amphitheatre that you have just crossed, trying to avoid the wet ground down the centre to your right and the rocky ground below Tavy Cleave Tor to your left.

C Tavy Cleave

The fast flowing Tavy, a recent river in geological terms, has cut a deep gorge into the moor. In time such deep, sharp gorges are broadened as debris is picked up by the river, but here the relative newness of the gorge means unsmooth edges and a litter of boulder debris close to the river.

d From Ger Tor, instead of diverting to Tavy Cleave Tors (as in c), it is possible to undertake a longer walk, but on a higher grade (3 rather than 2) because of the rocky character of the upper end of Tavy Cleave. From Ger Tor, continue north, then north-east on the Lane End Track (HARVEY), to Deadlake (559841), bearing right to Deadlake Foot (562840). Follow the flat right (W) bank of the Rattlebrook south to its confluence with the Tavy, and continue south-west on the rough tracks above the river, through rocks and boulders, some involving clambering (easy if dry), until under the Tavy Cleave Tors.

e Continue along the west bank of the Tavy until you join the mine leat crossed on the outward journey (550830). Follow this south-west contouring around Nattor Down, with Nattor Farm down to the left, to reach the bridge crossed on the ascent to Ger Tor. From here, reverse the outward route.

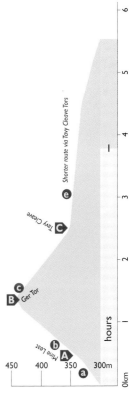

GREAT MIS TOR

MAPS:
Harvey Dartmoor South, OS
Landranger Sheet 191, OS
Outdoor Leisure Sheet 28

START/FINISH:
There are several car parks
along the B3357 between
Rundlestone and Merrivale, but
the best start is the Four Winds
park at 561749 on the
southern side of the road

DevonBuses 98, 98A and 172
all stop at Merrivale and Two
Bridges

DISTANCE/ASCENT:
5 miles (8km)/800ft (245m)

APPROXIMATE TIME:
2½ hours

HIGHEST POINT:
Great Mis Tor 1,765ft (538m)

REFRESHMENTS:
Two Bridges, Merrivale and
Princetown

ADVICE:
A clear track to Great Mis Tor
followed by rougher walking
on the way to Langstone Moor.
In poor weather the section
north of Great Mis Tor should
be avoided

This walk lies within one of the
Army's Dartmoor Firing Ranges.
Please read the section on the
ranges (see pp.9–10) before
setting out

As it nears Merrivale, the road from Two Bridges/Princetown to Tavistock (the B3357) is dominated by Great Mis Tor the last of northern Dartmoor's big peaks: to the south of the B3357, there is no peak higher than Great Mis. This walk climbs it for a fine view of the northern wilderness, visiting some fascinating old sites on the return.

A   Four Winds Car Park
When the granite quarries to the south of the road were active (see Note to Walk 12) there was a school for the children of the quarrymen on the spot now occupied by the car park.

a   Cross the B3357 with care, going half right to the obvious military road, which can be followed all the way to Little Mis Tor. However, as the tors ahead point the way, you can use the grass track which runs parallel to and on the right of the military road, and leading onto good moorland with plenty of sheep tracks where you can make your own route. Rejoin the military road just before reaching the distinctive granite cuboid of Little Mis Tor (564763), and enter the Merrivale Range (565764). Continue on strong tracks north-north-west to Great Mis Tor (563769), keeping to its west side.

B   Great Mis Tor
From the 13th century Great Mis Tor has been one of the southern boundary markers of the Dartmoor Forest, marking the point at which the parish of Walkhampton met the forest boundary.

It is said that the name derives from the mists which often envelope the peak. Unlikely as this seems it might well be true because the peak has long been used as a weather forecaster (the local piece of seaweed as it were) because of the tendency for clouds to reach it before they cloak the northern moor, probably because of its height and the tendency of local weather to arrive from the south-west.

The peak is a superb place, a maze of tors and boulders. The castle-like blocks (one topped by a range flag pole), all have relatively easy ascent routes on at least one side. The exception is the perched block, a giant weathered egg. From the tor the view north and north-east is marvellous, the real

Dartmoor of trackless wilderness, a succession of bogs and shallow valleys backed by the high northern tors.

Great Mis Tor would be worth visiting for the view alone, but also has a very good example of a rock basin, Mistorpan – found on top of the southern tor. As explained elsewhere (see Note to Walk 6), such basins are created by natural erosion processes. Here the corrosive hollowing has created a basin about 3ft (1m) across and about 8in (20cm) deep. On the southern edge of the basin a groove has been worn in the surrounding rock and this, of course, has been the basis of speculation about ancient sacrificial rituals, with blood collected in the basin running out along the groove. There is no evidence to support this (indeed, there is almost no evidence of such rituals in Neolithic or Bronze Age societies), but Dartmoor has never been a place where facts have been allowed to get in the way of a good horror story. Interestingly, though, local folklore does not seem to have incorporated the basin into a bloodthirsty tale; the story is from a later, more enlightened (?) age. In Dartmoor lore after the Devil and his Wisht hounds had chased the souls of sinners across the moor

Great Mis Tor from the River Walkham

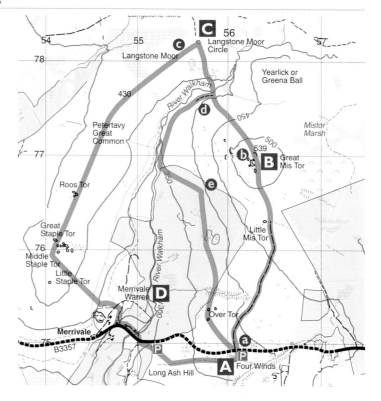

and cornered them in nearby Wistman's Wood (see Walk 5), the Devil would retire to Great Mis Tor and enjoy a fry-up breakfast made in the Devil's Frying Pan.

b   From Great Mis Tor, head north-north-west, descending through its boulder fields towards the valley of the River Walkham, aiming for the far bank at a point (559777) in line with the stone circle beyond, on top of open ground (559782), though steering a straight line while threading your way through rocks and clitter can be tricky! At the crossing point the bed rocks are flattish, but do not attempt the crossing if the river is too high or the rocks look slippery – see para d. After crossing, go half left ahead to visit the Bronze Age settlement on Langstone Moor (555780).

C   Langstone Moor and Merrivale Antiquities

The northern side of the Walkham Valley was the site of several Bronze Age settlements. Extending east and west from 559779 are a number of hut circles (see Note to Walk 7), and there is another group to the east where the Dead Lake stream reaches the River Walkham. To the north of the larger settlement (the one at 556779) is a stone circle, possibly associated with the folk from the village. The circle was restored in the 19th century and from the accounts of that times it seems it was D-shaped rather than a pure circle. It was about 60ft (18m) across and comprised about 16 stones. The speculative nature of size, shape and number of stones dates from the 1939–45 War when, sadly, the site was used as a practice target by troops training for the European theatre. They were fairly successful, reducing the circle to just a handful of stones.

The moor's name derives from another megalithic feature, the tall standing stone – the 'lang' or long stone at 550787 – to the north-west of the circle. The standing stone is set at the southern end of a short double row of stones that is aligned due north-south. The row once comprised 26–30 stones, but here too the army used them for target practice, reducing the number to about a dozen.

To the south of the BB3357 there is an expanse of large rocks where you can see the remains of several Iron Age walls, an unfinished giant mill wheel and some distinct hut circles.

c   Having crossed the river once you may prefer not to recross, in which case continue up to the ridge, heading south-west, and on from Langstone Moor to Roos Tor (1,489ft/454m) where we leave the Merrivale Range, continuing to Great Staple Tor (1,492ft/455m) and Middle Staple Tor (540757). From here go down left (SE 120°). The way is trackless, but over easy ground, and crosses a leat (547754) near the quarry corner, which you round to the right to pass through a gap between the quarry and the other enclosures, emerging by a telephone box. Then follow the old road left (E) past the Dartmoor Inn, continuing to the end of the road and ascending steeply up to the B3357. Cross carefully and take the small track under the wall between the farm entrance and the road fencing, leading you to a wall corner where you are on open moor. Bear right (SE) away from the road to see the Merrivale Antiquities (see Note to Walk 12), passing the double stone row, and following the brook eastwards to the car park.

D   Grimstone and Sortridge Leat
About ½ mile (800m) from the crossing point of the Walkham a leat is cut from the river's far bank. This point is the headweir of the Grimstone and Sortridge Leat. It is thought that the leat originally supplied water to farms and houses near Sampford Spinney and dates from the 15th century.

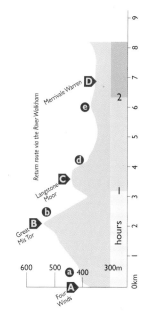

Please note: time taken calculated according to the Naismith Formula (see p.2)

From Great Mis Tor looking south-west

Later it provided water to local tin mines and to the Merrivale Quarry.

d Should you be unable or not wish to cross the river, follow the left (E) bank of the River Walkham southwards, noticing the prominent leat across the Walkham and occasionally branching along the hillside to avoid rocky areas, until you see a stile over a wall ahead. Before reaching the wall and stile, take the obvious track half left (SE 140°) to continue uphill towards the wall (which climbs towards the right-hand side of Great Mis Tor) and look for a second stile alongside a gate (555769).

In mist it would be better to use the wall as a guideline, staying on its left (moor) side, and following it round south-east, then south (as it turns away from Great Mis Tor). As it bends south-west (the fifth stile from the river end is just around a corner at 562762), turn east and walk about 180 yards (200m) to the military road below Little Mis Tor, for the car park below.

D Walkham Settlement and Merrivale Warren

To the west are the remains of the Walkham Settlement, another Bronze Age village. There are the remains of two dozen or so huts, one of them significantly larger than the others. It is assumed that this was occupied by the head man of the village. To the south of the main settlement there are more hut circles and the remains of boundary walls.

Also to the west are the ruins of a more substantial blowing house. There are also several pillow mounds which were part of the extensive Merrivale Warren.

As noted elsewhere (see Note to Walk 5), the Dartmoor tin miners constructed artificial mounds for rabbits to settle. The Merrivale Warren was one of the most extensive on the moor, supplying not only the tin miners but, later, the quarrymen with meat. The rabbits were caught by netting some of the Warren's tunnels and using dogs to chase the rabbits into the nets. The rabbit skins were sold to furriers at the edge of the moor. The warren was worked by a warrener who not only caught, dispatched and skinned the rabbits, but kept the number of rabbit predators – stoats and weasels – in check by setting traps.

e Cross over the stile (555769) and walk south-south-east (150°) on good grass, keeping well above the bracken cover to the right, passing many old enclosures and stone circles on this history-soaked land. Where the hillside begins to bear to the right, becoming quite rough and bush-covered, maintain direction and ultimately bear slightly left to reach a stile in the wall (at 559757). Cross the stile and turn right to follow the wall south-west on smooth grass, then crossing a wide gully and climbing towards a large, flat-topped rock on a small, rocky hillside (558754). Once clear of the rocks, head south-east over good ground to the car park.

The moorland Walkham valley stretching northward from Great Mis Tor

THE WEST DART RIVER & HIGHER WHITE TOR

MAPS:
Harvey Dartmoor North and Dartmoor South, OS Landranger Sheet 191, OS Outdoor Leisure Sheet 28

START/FINISH:
At 609751 the car park in the old quarry opposite the Two Bridges Hotel

Two Bridges is on the route of DevonBuses 98 (Totnes to Plymouth via Exeter, Moretonhampstead and Princetown), 98 (Tavistock to Bellever) and 172 (Totnes to Tavistock via Widecombe and Princetown)

DISTANCE/ASCENT:
6 miles (9.5km)/650ft (200m)

APPROXIMATE TIME:
3 hours

HIGHEST POINT:
Higher White Tor 1,729ft (527m)

REFRESHMENTS:
The Two Bridges Hotel; also at Princetown

ADVICE:
Straightforward in good weather and usually dry under foot, but care needed in poor visibility. Often boggy on the high ground

Close to Princetown is Two Bridges where the B3212 crosses the West Dart River. The walk north from there, following the river, reaches a superb viewpoint as well as passing a surprising section of woodland and the site of the moor's Stannary Parliament.

A Two Bridges

There is so little at Two Bridges it barely warrants the title of hamlet. The bridge over the West Dart River was the meeting point of the two cross-moor turnpike roads whose routes are now followed by the B3212 and the B3357, and in Victorian times the hotel was used to accommodate those taking guided walks on the moor. To the south of Two Bridges was the Tor Royal house and estate of Sir Thomas Tyrwhitt (see Notes to Walk 12). The car park opposite the hotel lies in an old granite quarry.

a   Go through the gate at the moor end of the car park and either follow a clear, but stony, track northwards, bearing to the right by the farmhouse, then continuing north at a higher level to a waymarked stile (612758); or, far better, immediately after the gate by the car park, bear right up a small path leading to grassy access land, over which you can make your own route. The best way is to head north-north-east until passing the gorse level, then to flatten out and head north,

The West Dart Valley with Wistman's Wood

Inside Wistman's Wood

keeping just left of the hill ridge and parallel to the farm track, going through a gateway in a wall (611754), passing pillow mounds by the edge of the gorse above the farmhouse (the roof can be seen from the hillside). Then, with the main path ahead of you, make for the signpost a little below, and join the main path, to cross the next wall by the waymarked stile (612758); Wistman's Wood can be seen ahead.

B   Pillow Mounds

Not related to the geological process that produces pillow lava, pillow mounds found on Dartmoor have been man-made to attract rabbits. The domed earth mounds offered the animals a dry and easily burrowed site and warrens of healthy rabbits were rapidly established. The rabbits were then caught and eaten by the local tin miners or farmers who had constructed the mound. The empathy the tin miners had for the rabbit which, like them, lived part of its life underground, and which provided them with a valuable source of food, was such that the miners took a circle of rabbits as their emblem. The emblem can be seen in carved roof bosses in the churches at North Bovey and Widecombe-in-the-Moor. On the OS maps of Dartmoor 'Pillow Mound' is usually written in the Gothic script reserved for prehistoric sites, but it is not thought that they date back that far. Trowlesworthy Warren, for instance, dates back to 1272. The most famous of Eden Phillpotts' Dartmoor Cycle of novels – based on the moor and characters that Phillpotts (who died in 1960) knew – is *The River* which concerns the tragic love affair of a rabbit catcher working the pillow mounds from a hut near Wistman's Wood and the daughter of the Two Bridges Inn.

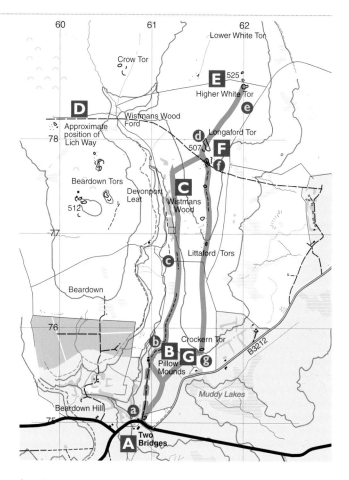

b Continue north along the clear, main path towards Wistman's Wood, until reaching another wall and a stile over it (613767). The display board is of interest.

C Wistman's Wood

There are three copses of oak remaining on upland Dartmoor: Black-a-Tor copse in the West Okement Valley below Black Tor (near Yes Tor – see Walk 9); Piles Copse beside the River Erme below Harford Moor (see Walk 27); and here in the West Dart's valley. Each lies above the 900ft (275m) contour and has been protected from grazing animals by the boulder heaps in which it grows. All three copses are believed to be remnants of Dartmoor's original tree cover. Wistman's Wood is by far the most interesting of the three, its trees – as with the other copses they are mostly pedunculate (English) oaks – gnarled and stunted, limited in height by the bitter winter winds which sweep across the valley. The copse is extremely important ecologically, not only for the trees, but for the ferns, mosses and lichens that live on them and the mosses that grow on the boulders between them. The wood is home to *Bryoria smithii*, a rare lichen which, in Britain, grows only here and in Black-a-Tor Copse. The bent, twisted trees are also very romantic, making Wistman's Wood a delightful spot.

The romance could hide a sinister truth, some saying that the copse's name derives from the 'Wisht' hounds that the Devil used to hunt the moor for the souls of sinners. The hounds chased the souls to the copse where they would become trapped by the boulders and bent branches – easy pickings for the pursuing dogs. But there is another, less sinister, idea for the origin of the name, some believing it derives from an ancient Celtic name. Maen is stone in Welsh (Celtic), while wystn means stump. This could then be stump stone wood, an apt description.

c After crossing the stile, continue northwards until the path divides, about 220 yards (200m) before the woods. Here take the right fork, on a clear main path, still heading north, but climbing slightly and aiming for a point a little to the right of and above the woods. Continue along this easy path, keeping a little above the woods most of the way, until the path passes alongside and close to part of the woods towards the northern end – giving an excellent view of the moss-covered boulders and the lichen-festooned interior of Wistman's Wood. The clear path continues north and arrives just above the final section of the wood, where there is a large area of rock boulders.

Continue north for approximately 80 yards (70m) past the end of the woods, mostly on grass, until you come towards the end of another bouldery area, where there is a large, chest-shaped rock just to the right of the path. Continue north on the main path for another 33 yards (30m) when another large, but flatter, rock lies to the right. Here you turn right, east-north-east, along a small path up the hillside to Longaford Tor. Care is required here, as forward, the main path continues out to wild moorland and there is a distinct change in the vegetation pattern. Just ahead you will also see another area of boulders and three old trees, which you keep on your left as you ascend towards Longaford Tor. Shortly before reaching the tor (616779), you cross the Lich Way where a few of the rocks now carry blue waymarks.

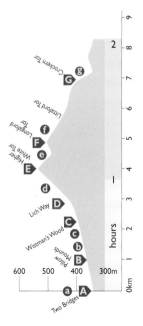

Please note: time taken calculated according to the Naismith Formula (see p.2)

D Lich Way

In the days when feet and horses were the only moorland transport, the bodies of the recently deceased had to be carried across the moor from outlying farms to Lydford churchyard (most of Dartmoor is in the Parish of Lydford). The Lich Way – from lich, the old word for a corpse – can still be traced for much of its length. From the northern end of Wistman's Wood it follows the West Dart north, then crosses the river and heads west to Lydford Tor before turning north-west towards Lydford. The Way is said to be haunted by a procession of white clad monks.

d Continue to the west side of Longaford Tor, noting its dragon-like formation, then go to the northern end of the rocks. Higher White Tor (620786) is in view and the energetic can take the distinct track in a north-easterly direction to reach the tor, returning the same way.

E Higher White Tor

From the tor there is a fine view northward over Dartmoor's wildest section. To the north-west are Devil's Tor and Rough Tor – worthy objectives for another day, while to the west is the plateau of Black Dunghill (such an evocative name!) with Great Mis Tor beyond. To the south-east Bellever Tor stands above the conifer forest south of Postbridge. To the north of Higher White Tor, Brown's House is one of the remotest of all Dartmoor farms. Now ruinous, it is said to be named for an old farmer who chose its site because of the youth and beauty of his wife, fearing losing her to younger men if they saw her.

e Retrace your steps to Longaford Tor passing a small stone row on your left (SE) – a ruined double row, one of the highest on Dartmoor. Continue along the eastern side of the tor from where there is a fine panorama of the tors to the south-east, with Bellever Forest in view and the chimney of Powder Mills (so-called because there was a gunpowder mill there in the last half of the 19th century) in the valley.

F Longaford Tor

On the approach to Longaford Tor from the west side you will see a dragon-like head in the rock. Although created by natural erosion, legend has it that the dragon sleeps within the tor, only its rock-like head exposed and that at night it wanders the local moor catching and eating solitary folk.

f Now head south descending gently to Littaford Tors. From the final prominent tor continue descending to the ladder stile in the wall of Crockern Newtake marked 'Permitted Access'. Maintaining direction south, but moving gradually more to the west of the wall on your left, descend to Crockern Tor, which will only come into sight just before you reach it.

G   Crockern Tor

In addition to the Stannary Courts which dealt with offenders against the laws of the tin miners (see Note to Walk 1) there was also a Stannary Parliament which met on an ad hoc basis to consider the need for regulations affecting the industry. The Parliament consisted of 96 stannators, 24 from each of the districts of Tavistock, Chagford, Ashburton and Plympton. The sittings were very irregular; ten are known to have take nplace between 1494 and 1703. The representatives met here at Crockern Tor, chosen as it was at the geographical centre of the various mines. It is said that slabs were carved out of the granite of the tor for the representatives to sit on, but no evidence of this survives. On the south-west side of the tor a rock formation does look a little like a giant chair and is occasionally known as the Judge's Chair or Parliament Rock. The tor is also said to be haunted by a rider on a skeleton horse.

g   From Crockern Tor head down west towards the outward path, but do not go as far as the stile in the wall; make for a gateway about 110 yards (100m) to the left of the stile. Pass through the gateway and keep along the right hand side of the small ridge, remembering the gateway in the next wall (611754), used on the way out. Continue until reaching the end wall to the south; when this comes into view, bear right and downhill, towards an old farm structure, making for the gate through which you started.

The tinner's Parliament Rock on Crockern Tor

SHOVEL AND SCORHILL DOWN

MAPS:
Harvey Dartmoor North, OS Landranger Sheet 191, OS Outdoor Leisure Sheet 28

START/FINISH:
There is a car park at 661878, at the end of the minor road from Berrydown to Scorhill Farm. Parking is also possible at 662866 at the end of the road from Teigncombe to Batworthy.

The start is not on any bus route. DevonBus 174 (Okehampton to Moretonhampstead) stops at Chagford which lies to the east of the route.

DISTANCE/ASCENT:
5½ miles (9km)/600ft (180m)

APPROXIMATE TIME:
3 hours

HIGHEST POINT:
Shovel Down 1,420ft (433m)

REFRESHMENTS:
None on the walk, but available in Chagford 3 miles (5km) to the west

ADVICE:
A straightforward walk over moorland and along minor roads and forest tracks; going can be wet from the teign to Batworthy Corner. However, the moorland section is featureless and needs care in poor visibility

To the west of Chagford the River Teign, flowing down from the central moor near Quintin's Man, splits the moor into two high downs, each topped by interesting megalithic monuments. This walk explores the two, linking them by crossing the river over one of Dartmoor's most evocatively named clapper bridges.

a   From the car park, head west-south-west across the moor walking between stone walls. When the wall on the left bears away, bear slightly left (SW), gently uphill over the low rise ahead. Maintain direction across the high plateau, passing a barely discernible hut circle – probably Bronze Age, the huts consisted of a circle of stones, most likely with a central pole to hold up a conical roof of poles covered with skins or turf. Continue across the moor to the Scorhill stone circle (655874).

A   Scorhill Stone Circle

Scorhill is one of the finest of all Dartmoor's stone circles. Folk lore claims that the exact number of stones cannot be counted as the fairy folk move them as you are attempting the count. It is also unique in never having been restored, though it has often been robbed: close by several of the stones have been used to create the channel of the leat which fed water from Gallaven Mire to the village of Gidleigh: the leat is crossed to the south of the circle.

Looking south-east from Scorhill Drift Lane

The circle is almost 80ft (25m) in diameter and comprises about 25 stones, the tallest about 7ft (over 2m) in height. The circle is very romantically sited, the view west being the essence of Dartmoor, with the bleak and boggy plain of the North Teign River backed by Western Tor and Hangingstone Hill.

Part of the magnificent Bronze-Age stone circle of Scorhill

This area of Dartmoor was clearly important in late Neolithic/early Bronze Age. To the north of Scorhill Down, on Buttern Hill, there is another stone circle, smaller and less attractive than Scorhill, and a number of hut circles, while to the north-east, on the southern slope of Kennon Hill there are the remains of a large Bronze Age settlement.

b   From the circle, head south, crossing the Walla Brook clapper bridge (653871) to reach the clapper bridge at Teign-e-ver (654871).

B   Teign-e-ver Clapper Bridge
Teign-e-ver is another of Dartmoor's romantic features, the more so for being in such a lonely section of the moor. Amazingly, for being so lonely there is actually another clapper just a short distance to the north-west, over Walla Brook. The Walla Brook's course was straightened by the moor's tin miners to increase its flow rate and, therefore, its usefulness to them as a means of 'streaming' tin ore (see Note to Walk 24). It is conjectured that the tin miners built both the Walla Brook and Teign clappers to gain access to Scorhill Down from the Teigncombe side of the river. Teign-e-ver was rebuilt in 1826 when a flood destroyed an earlier version, and has been reconstructed more recently (1999).

Close to Teign-e-ver, a short distance downstream, is the Teign Tolmen, a curious holed stone. Such holes are occasionally carved naturally by the stream – the process of hole carving is seen, in glorious fashion in the Lydford Gorge on Walk 1 – and seem to have been of great significance to the megalith builders. Men-an-Tol, on Cornwall's Penwith Moor consists of two upright stones with the holed stone between them, a clear fertility symbol. There is evidence that until quite recently babies were passed through the hole as a way of ensuring their good health. Here the Tolmen is occasionally referred to as the Christianity Stone, implying a similar rite. It is also said to ease the symptoms of rheumatism sufferers who crawl through the hole.

The wild valley of the Teign to the west of Teign-e-ver is the occasional haunt of the merlin, one of Britain's rarest falcons.

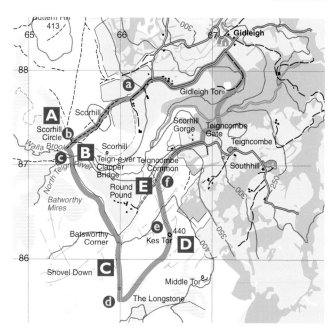

c   From Teign-e-ver, follow the wall on the left (but keep well away from the wet area), to reach Batworthy Corner (660862) where the wall, behind which is Batworthy House, turns sharply back left having reached its southern extremity. Now walk south to reach the stone rows and other megalithic monuments on Shovel Down – the now-accepted name for a section of moor which has also been called Shuggledown and Shuffledown. Keep well away from the wall to the south where the bog can be dangerous.

C   Shovel Down

For number and complexity the megalithic monuments on the Down are the equal of those at Merrivale, though they are much less famous. There are five stone rows here, a stone circle and several single standing stones. As some of the stones cannot be seen from others, it is thought that the site represents not one complex, but a series of unrelated (though clearly not completely unrelated: they are, after all, on the same piece of moorland) sites. Some of the rows have been robbed of their stones by wall builders and gate hangers, but are still impressive. The most northerly row, which has lost many of its stones, is about 200 yards (180m) long and ends in a series of four standing stones which are thought to have formed a tomb. The row points due north, while the two nearby rows are angled away at about 25°. The southerly row is the most impressive, ending at a large standing stone called the Longstone. South again is a single stone called the Three Boys, its curious title arising from the fact that once there were indeed three stones, but two were plundered to act as gateposts. The southern row also points due north. At its northern end it is crossed at an angle by a row of single stones (all the other rows are of double stones) which has a curious dog-leg about one-third of the way along its length.

d From the megaliths head north-east across Chagford Common to reach the high point of Kes Tor (665862).

D Kes Tor

At the summit of Kes Tor is a curious rock basin, once thought to have been carved by prehistoric man, perhaps to capture blood during some sacrificial ritual, but now known to be the result of natural weathering. The erosion process is similar to that which creates pot holes in stream beds. A natural hollow in the rock collects water which, because rainwater is slightly acidic, due to its swirling in the wind and, perhaps, by freezing and thawing causes crystals of mica to be removed from the rock. Over countless years, the swirling action of the mica in water acts as a shot blaster causing the basin to be cut. The erosion process preferentially attacks weaker areas in the rock, sometimes causing weird shapes to be carved: on Bodmin Moor, over the border in Cornwall, one basin is in the outline of a man. Here on Kes Tor the more usual circular basin has been carved. There is another basin at Middle Tor to the south-east.

The Teign-e-ver stone clapper bridge over the North Teign

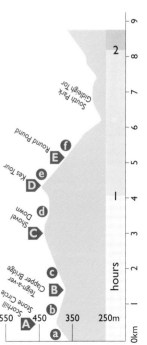

Prehistoric stone rows on Shovel Down

Looking north from Kes Tor, even the untrained eye can see curious ridges running north-east/south-west and the occasional circle of stones. These are the remains of a fairly extensive Bronze Age settlement, the stone circles being the bases of a series of huts, the shallow ridges being 'reaves', low stone walls which defined the edges of fields. Excavations of the site revealed several thousand stone age implements, proving that the area had a long history of settlement. But much more interesting was the discovery, during an excavation in the 1950s, of evidence of iron smelting. Experts are still divided on the meaning of discovery. Does it imply a natural progression from Bronze to Iron Age, a possibility which seems denied by the accepted view that the metal was brought to Britain from Europe by early Celts, or does it simply mean that later iron-using folk merely used a convenient ruin they found on the moor as a base for their work?

e   From Kes Tor, head north-north-west, descending through the Bronze Age settlement to reach a road near Round Pound (at 664868).

E   Round Pound
The pound looks almost fortress-like, its walls massive enough to have persuaded the road builders to deflect around it, rather than to demolish it. It is likely that the pound dates from the late Bronze Age, though as one of the reaves of the Bronze Age settlement runs beneath it this cannot be taken as fact. The pound consists of a central hut surrounded by a walled enclosure. This is now divided into five 'paddocks', several with exits on to the moor, though it is not clear whether this is the work of a latter occupant. It is likely that the pound was used by medieval shepherds and perhaps even by tinners so the paddocks and their entranceways could be much younger than the main structure. As elsewhere (see Note to Walk 7) the true purpose is still debated, though here the existence of earlier, or contemporary, reaves seems to imply the coralling of domestic animals.

f   From the pound follow the road north-eastwards, bearing right (and downhill) with it to reach, after about ½ mile (800m), a sharp right turn (669873). Here turn left along a wide track. The track forms part of the Mariners' Way, a historic long-distance footpath linking Dartmouth with Bideford. It is said to be a late medieval route, once followed by sailors walking between the two ports in search of new ships to join. Follow the track through the fine woodland of

The Tolmen Stone with its huge natural hole

Gidleigh Park, around a sharp right-hand bend, and take the left fork (ENE). The path descends steeply to reach the River Teign. Cross the footbridge and bear right (NE) along a path climbing through more woodland. The path first climbs steeply, then flattens out as it rounds Gidleigh Tor (hidden by trees): continue NW close to the wood edge to reach a minor road at 672883. Turn left and follow the road SW through Berrydown, forking left just beyond the hamlet to return to the start.

GREY WETHERS STONE CIRCLE AND SANDY HOLE PASS

MAPS:
Harvey Dartmoor North, OS Landranger Sheets 191, OS Outdoor Leisure Sheet 28

START/FINISH:
There are two car parks at Postbridge, one at the National Park Centre (at 647789) on the north side of the B3212 and one on south side of the road, a little further away, at 646787

Postbridge lies on the route of DevonBus 82 and 98

DISTANCE/ASCENT:
8½ miles (13.5km)/750ft (230m)

APPROXIMATE TIME:
4 hours

HIGHEST POINT:
Statts House Hill (OS Winney's Down) ,765ft (538m)

REFRESHMENTS:
There is an inn at Postbridge

ADVICE:
A good introduction to walking on the high northern moor. The path beside the East Dart River is good and easy to follow, but the route to Grey Wethers and the crossing between Sittaford Tor and Statts House Hill are more difficult – pathless and boggy as well as wild

This walk lies on the edge of one of the Army's Dartmoor Firing Ranges. Please read the section on the ranges (pp.9–10) before setting out

Postbridge, a tiny collection of houses and a National Park information centre, is the start point for several fine walks. This one heads north, following the East Dart River and visiting one of the moor's best stone circles.

A Postbridge See Note to Walk 10

a From either car park follow the B3212 towards Moretonhampstead, crossing the bridge over the East Dart River. Just beyond the bridge, turn left through a gate and follow a waymarked and gated path to Ringhill Farm. The path bears left here, soon reaching the river. Now bear right, with the river on your left, passing Hartland Farm (on the right) and going through several gates to reach open country. The path is less distinct now, but the route is easy until a boggy area just before a rock outcrop is reached which necessitates a diversion slightly uphill around the outcrop, the path from here being at a higher level. This higher path is followed until the river is seen to begin a wide bend to the left, at which point (639813) it is joined by a brook flowing into it from the north. This is Ladehill Brook, and our route follows its east bank for about 50 yards (46m), to find, tucked away on our right, the Beehive Hut.

B Beehive Hut
The 'hut', a low circular wall of stones, is one of the best known features of the northern moor because of its closeness to Postbridge, yet there is no absolute consensus of opinion on it. Most experts believe it was a conical hut built by tinners to store their tools and equipment while they were off the moor. In answer to the query of why such apparently conspicuous huts were built to protect against theft, expert opinion claims that they were turfed over and probably looked similar to other features, the shape making them very weatherproof.

b From just above the Beehive Hut a clear path now follows the east side of the Ladehill Brook valley, heading almost due north, but keeping east of a marshy area. Sittaford Tor can be seen topping the hill ahead and to the left. As the end of the stream valley is reached, a few rocky mounds are visible. These are the poorly-preserved remains of hut circles (at

639825), though only two or three out of the 15 or so forming the settlement can be identified.

C   Hut Circles and Pounds

The climate of Bronze Age Britain was warmer and drier than today and Dartmoor was suitable for primitive agriculture and stock raising whereas today, few farms are found on the high moor. Aerial surveys indicate the existence of many thousands of hut circles, the base of Bronze Age huts. A conical roof – supported at its centre by a pole set in the floor – of branches covered with animal skins or turf rose from the low circular wall. The huts were floored with slabs of stone. The hut walls were up to 3ft (1m) thick, the hut diameters varying from 10ft–30ft (3–10m). The huts are found in groups, as here, but also as single circles implying the existence of both village-type settlements and, perhaps, herders for sheep, goats and cattle. It is thought that in the groups, some huts were for living/sleeping, with others for cooking and food storage. Similar circles had no huts and these pounds are thought to have been used to prevent livestock trampling or eating crops. There is also evidence of a reave system – parallel stone and earth banks running for long distances, an aspect of Dartmoor that has come to light only recently as a result of detailed aerial surveys – which would imply large cultivated areas, as indeed would be expected.

The Beehive Hut near Ladehill Brook

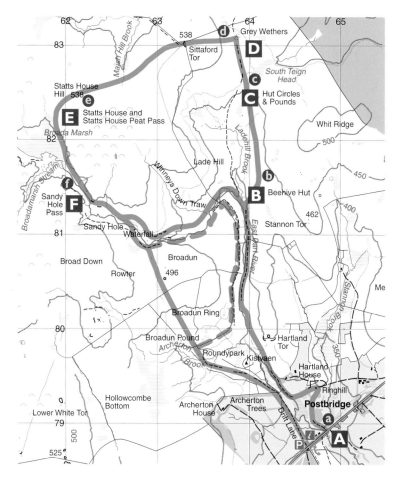

c Continue north from the hut circles to join a wider, well-trodden path which, cresting a rise, arrives at the Grey Wethers stone circle (at 639831).

D Grey Wethers

There are actually two stone circles, of approximately equal diameters (the southern circle is about 100ft (30.5m) across, the northern one a little smaller) lying almost exactly on a north-south line. The circles were restored in about 1900, many fallen stones being raised, so the exact form, and even the number of stones, is a matter of some conjecture. It is now thought that the northern circle had 18 or so stones, the southern one about 28. As there are no other stones, either singly or in rows, and no knowledge of the original (pre-restoration) form, no astronomical associations have been made for the circles. They are, therefore, a delightful enigma. The name reflects the fact that from a distance the stones look like grey sheep, the word 'wethers' being a West Country dialect word for sheep. There are other 'grey wethers' on Dartmoor, and the same name is given to the sarsens used to construct Avebury in Wiltshire. A local legend maintains that a confidence trickster once successfully sold this 'flock' to a gullible newcomer.

The fact that many of the Grey Wethers stones had fallen by 1900 sheds an interesting light on another local folk tale. It is said that a wife suspected of unfaithfulness would be taken to Cranmere Pool and forced to bathe in its cold, peaty waters, then taken to either the Scorhill stone circle (to the north-east near Teigncombe – see Walk 6) or brought here to Grey Wethers. She was then forced to kneel in front of a stone: if it fell on her she was guilty as charged, if not she was innocent. The tale maintains that the falling stone would crush the woman, but they seem hardly big enough. Such stories are interesting – how could the idea have ever taken root? And how could it have survived if a stone never actually fell at exactly the right moment? And what does the large number of fallen stones say about Dartmoor wives?

d   From the Grey Wethers walk on north for a few yards to reach a wall running from west to east. Turn west-south-west opposite a gate and follow the wall uphill to Sittaford Tor, a good viewpoint. North-westwards are Quintin's Man and Whitehorse Hill, with Fernworthy Forest's mass of conifers to the east. To the west are the wilds of Cut Hill/Black Hill with the East Dart River cutting its way across the moor to the south.

From the tor, climb a stile and follow the wall south-westwards for a few yards. As it elbows left, maintain direction (243°), following a narrow path in the direction of the high point of Statts House Hill (621826) (OS Winney's Down). Before reaching Statts House Hill it is necessary to negotiate (at 626827) a shallow and marshy valley which gives birth to the Marsh Hill Brook. Crossing this will require a diversion to the left of some 50–100 yards (46–91m) or more before climbing the tussocky slope of the hill, without an obvious path, to its summit, where Statts House sits and where a peat pass will be found.

E   Statts House and the Marsh Hill Peat Pass
Statts House is the ruin of an old peat-cutter's cottage or, though much less likely, a tin miner's cottage. The nearby peat

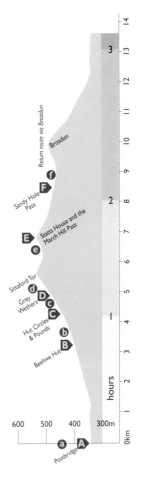

Sandy Hole Pass on the East Dart – evidence of the tinner's skills in channelling water

pass (also known as Statts House Cut) at 621825 is one of several cut by Frank Phillpotts, a Victorian gentleman who – as the plaque notes – died in 1909. Phillpotts cut the passes to help moormen, but chiefly hunters, negotiate more easily difficult sections of the moor. He cut down through the peat to the granite sub-strata, creating a good path for horses. His half-dozen or so passes are all marked – at each end – by memorial stones/plaques erected by his brother and son.

e   The upper end of the peat pass, unseen from the building remains is marked by a short granite post (at 621825) 90 paces to the north-west, bearing a plaque. Take care at this point as this section of the walk lies near the edge of the Okehampton Military Range, and this part of the moor is very wild, so careful navigation is required. The pass is shallow and not well defined, but a clear path south-west follows it to its lower end, marked by another post with a plaque. At this point bear half-left (S) along an indistinct path which edges round east of Broad Marsh to reach the East Dart River (at 619818, opposite Broad Marsh Stream). Turn left and follow the river through Sandy Hole Pass.

F   Sandy Hole Pass

The natural geography of the East Dart's valley confined the river to a narrow gorge here, but the moor's tinners built up the banks, narrowing the river still further and so increasing its flow rate. The river was then used to stream tin (see Note to Walk 24). A leat also took water to run a waterwheel. The increased flow rate also helped drain Broad Marsh which helped the miners work the river's tributary streams for tin ore. The Pass, named for the sand which accumulated in the river bed, is one of the most pleasant places on the northern moor on sunny days and often attracts a (small) crowd.

f   Follow the river south east through Sandy Hole Pass (620817–622813) to a broad, flat valley where the river bears east. Cut across the loop in the river (at 622812) keeping it on your right. A picturesque waterfall is soon reached (627811), at which the options are either to cross the large slabs above the fall if feasible and use a route south of the river; or to stay on the north (left) bank (see Walk 10 para e).

If you are staying on the north bank, the way from the waterfall follows a well-marked, elevated path contouring round above the river, then descends slowly to a gate in the wall at 636814. From here the way rejoins our outward route at the confluence of the East Dart and Ladehill Brook.

Crossing the brook proceed south and south east past Hartland Farm and Ringhill to Postbridge.

If you decide to cross the river at the waterfall, the alternatives are described in Walk 10 (paras f and g). In short, take the upper path heading south east avoiding the rock debris below the waterfall as far as the next bend in the river (628209) where, after crossing an inlet, the paths fork and there are two choices. Either take the clear path ascending south east/south-south-east, continuing to the trig. point 1,627ft/496m on Broadun, maintain direction and cross the stile. Follow the (permitted) path down south-south-east (to 634800), then cross Braddon Lake, continuing almost to the west bank of the East Dart (643794). A good track follows to the Park Centre.

Alternatively, if desired, it is possible to follow the south bank round east, initially following the strong path eastwards over the foothills to avoid steep ground, but descending to follow the riverside path as the river bends north east and you are in sight of rockier foothills and a line of wall crossing the river (stile at 637813) before the river turns south east opposite the Beehive. From here follow the contouring path south and south-west to the stile above Braddon Lake, then Drift Lane on towards the car park.

The impressive East Dart Falls near Sandy Hole Pass

BELSTONE AND COSDON

MAPS:
Harvey Dartmoor North, OS
Landranger Sheet 191, OS
Outdoor Leisure Sheet 28

START/FINISH:
Belstone village, reached by
minor roads from the A30 or
from Okehampton. There is a
car park on Brenamoor
Common at the northern end
of the village (621938)

DevonBus 670 on Mondays
and Thursdays, stops at
Belstone Post Office

DISTANCE/ASCENT:
10 miles (16km)/1,200ft
(380m)

APPROXIMATE TIME:
5 hours

HIGHEST POINT:
Cosdon Beacon 1,804ft (550m)

REFRESHMENTS:
The Tors Inn, Belstone and The
Barton, a tea garden. There are
also numerous possibilities in
nearby Okehampton

ADVICE:
A strenuous walk with difficult
terrain in its southern section.
Unless proficient in use of map
and compass, do not attempt
this walk in poor visibility

This walk lies within one of
the Army's Dartmoor Firing
Ranges. Please read the
section on the ranges
(pp.9–10) before setting out

A t the extreme northern end of the National Park, to the south-east of Okehampton are the massive hills of Belstone and Cosdon. This route climbs both, linking them by heading south to cross one of the wildest sections of the moor.

A   Belstone

This pretty little village is grouped around two greens; on one stand the old stocks. Nearby is St Mary's Church, originally built in the 15th century, but rebuilt in the 1880s. The church has a famous peal of six bells. The old Zion Chapel, built in 1841, is now the Post Office.

a   From the car park walk westwards through the centre of the village, with the Post Office on your right and the Tors Inn on the left. Ignore the left turn for the church, continuing for about 55 yards (50m) taking the next lane on the left heading south-west (a 'No Through Road'). Walk past the Water Treatment Plant, on the right, continuing to the end of the lane. Go through the gate on to the moor, maintaining direction along a track which contours below Watchet Hill on the left, with a wall on the right. The wall bears away to the right, continue along the stony track for a further 200 yards (183m); a granite kerb crosses the track at this point, and you turn off left and south-south-east to reach the Nine Maidens Stone Circle.

B   Nine Maidens Stone Circle

There are now 16 stones in the circle, the naming having the curious eccentricity which is frequently applied to such sites. There is an alternative name, the Seventeen Brothers, which seems much closer to the mark. The legend behind the name is also one frequently heard, that the maidens (or the brothers) met here to dance on a Sunday and were turned to stone for their blasphemy. Interestingly, here the legend maintains that the stones come alive at noon each day to enjoy another dance. The truth of this is said to be that after they complete the dance the stones do not quite regain their original positions and that each day this change can be detected.

b   From the circle head south-east up to the tors at the northern edge of Belstone Common and continue past several more tors to reach Belstone Tor. Continue southwards to reach Irishman's Wall (613919).

C Irishman's Wall and Belstone Common

The wall crosses the summit plateau of Belstone Common, extending into the valleys on either side. It was built by the Irishmen of the name in an attempt to enclose a section of the common and was promptly attacked by folk from Belstone and Okehampton to ensure that the common remained open. However, there are two versions of how Irishmen came to be building a wall on Dartmoor. One maintains that they were Ulster Protestants driven from Ireland in the 17th century, while another claims they were 18th century labourers working for a local squire who intended to increase his land holding. Whichever is correct, it is certainly true that the intervention of local folk was decisive: after they had torn down sections of the wall it was never rebuilt.

Belstone Common is one of Dartmoor's finest sections of upland heath, home to the rare stag's horn clubmoss and the emperor moth. Winter walkers may also catch a glimpse of a merlin or hen harrier.

The stocks at Belstone

c   Continue south-south-west through the wall to reach Higher Tor at the southern end of Belstone Common. Here stunted rowan trees grow from cracks in the granite, a symbol of the tenacity of life. Beyond Higher Tor the ridge of moorland narrows; continue south along it, soon passing a grassy mound (611913) marked as 'Cairn' on the OS map. This is almost certainly a Bronze Age round barrow. You then pass Knattaborough (1,437ft/438m), shortly entering the Okehampton Range and ahead is Oke Tor (sometimes called Ock Tor) (613901). A reasonable grass track follows the ridge line to the tor, from where there are fine views west to Yes Tor and High Willhays, Dartmoor's highest peaks.

From Oke Tor a military track heads south; follow it downhill into the Steeperton Gorge to reach a ford of the River Taw.

Nine Maiden's stone circle, near Belstone, with a view to Yes Tor

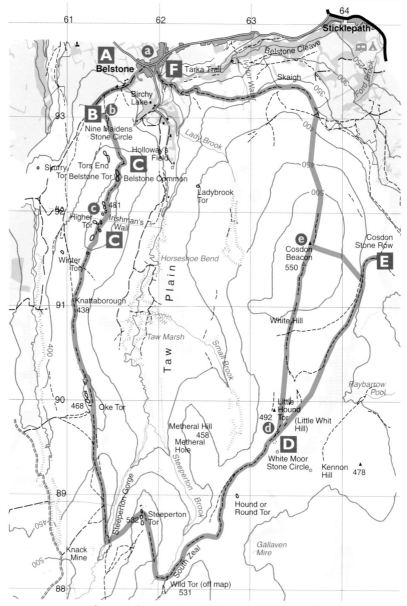

close to the remains of the Knack Mine, a tin mine active in the 19th century (the mine is about 150 yards (140m) upstream of the ford). The mine's name is a nice curio: the miners referred to the crushing or stamping of tin ore as knacking, but also referred to worked-out mines as being 'knacked'.

From the other side of the ford (614885) a path climbs steeply north-eastwards out of the gorge to the summit of Steeperton Tor (618888). Steeperton is one of the most mountainous of all Dartmoor's tors, with a steep-sided, elliptical peak rather than the more usual plateau-like summit. From it, follow the rough path heading south-south-east towards Wild Tor, going downhill to a ford of Steeperton Brook (620881). Beyond the ford, follow the path north-north-eastwards, climbing away from the stream. After a few yards you will see the ruins of a tin miner's hut to your left across the brook. Shortly we leave the Okehampton Range.

Follow the path as it contours north-north-east around Hound Tor (629890). A detour is required to reach the summit of this tor which is much higher, but much less famous than its namesake near Widecombe. At the base of the shallow climb to Little Hound Tor the path divides: take the right branch north-east, and quickly a small path to the right, to reach the White Moor Stone Circle (632896).

D White Moor Stone Circle

This evocative circle, with a diameter of about 66ft (20m), comprises about 16 stones, though as elsewhere the true number when it was first constructed is a matter of conjecture as it is known that locals took stones for building work and the Victorian restorers who raised many fallen stones may have altered not only the positions but added a few. As with Nine Maidens, the restoration has destroyed any possible astronomical alignments the circle may have had. To the south-east of the circle is a tall (5½ft/1.7m) standing stone which marks the junction of three parishes. It is possible that the stone is ancient and was incorporated into the parish boundaries because of its convenience. But it is also possible that it was moved from the circle to act as a boundary marker.

Knack Mine Ford in the rugged Steeperton gorge

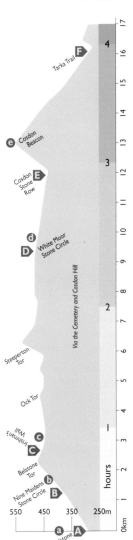

Please note: time taken calculated according to the Naismith Formula (see p.2)

The summit of Cosdon Beacon looking south

d From the circle the route depends upon the desires of the walker. To see The Cemetery, the stone row on Cosdon Hill's eastern flank (at 644916), continue along the bridleway north-north-east past the circle. The bridleway contours around Cosdon Hill, passing the row on its way to South Zeal. To continue over Cosdon, take the small path right off the bridleway, south-west of the stone row.

To go directly to the summit of Cosdon Hill, take the path from the path junction (at 632897) which goes straight on (N) towards Little Hound Tor. The path over Little Hound Tor descends to a shallow col, then heads up Cosdon Hill to reach the cairn-topped summit. The cairns are Bronze Age, but Neolithic flint tools have also been found here. For many years the fact that Cosdon Hill dominates the northern skyline of Dartmoor led people to believe it was the moor's highest peak. At 1,804ft (550m) it is actually 285ft (69m) lower than High Willhays.

E Cosdon Stone Row (The Cemetery)

This superb triple stone row runs almost due east-west, implying an alignment with the rising and setting sun. The rows are about 150 yards (140m) long and comprise dozens of stones not apparently chosen to be equal in shape or height (though as with many moorland megalithic sites the rows have been restored). At the western end of the rows there is evidence of a small stone circle and most certainly a kistvaen. Kistvaens are burial boxes formed from four small slabs of stones, usually topped by another slab acting as a lid, the whole often earthed over. The box would have originally contained the cremated remains of a body. Perhaps the kistvaen led to the row being called The Cemetery (or, sometimes, The Graveyard) locally: there seems to be no other reason for the name.

e From the summit of Cosdon a well-used track makes for a pile of rocks on a bearing of 30° (just east of north) and then descends generally north. Three walls are used as markers on the descent: the first at the point where the ground flattens out under Cosdon and the tracks meet the contouring bridleway round its base, our target being the left-hand corner of a wall (at 638931) to the north-east. The tracks divide below a stunted tree (left), the stronger route heading north-east well to the right of the wall corner. Our route is the fainter track to the north, veering east of north. If you miss the turning (eg in mist) you will simply meet the wall lower down. Descend towards the wall, meeting another track at a

T-junction. Turn left and north-west, then quickly right (N) over a wet area, still aiming for the left-hand corner of the wall. As you reach it (638931), cross over other tracks and continue north-west on the same line as the wall, heading across grass, towards a clump of gorse, and contouring round on a horse track veering gradually west, to the wall corner above Skaigh Warren to the left of a line of trees (634933).

From here we contour a few yards west-south-west, with the bank which continues in line with the wall on our right. By the tall boundary stone marked 'DC', fork right going gently downhill (W) on a well-defined track which eventually steepens towards the Taw. We meet our third wall (on the right) and continue alongside until a corner, where there is a gate on the right. Here do not follow the obvious track ahead, but bear left through the bushes, initially on grass, on the direct track down to the bridge over the Taw (621933), now on the Tarka Trail, and up to Belstone.

E   Tarka Trail
The ancient name for a river in Devon was Ta, explaining its use as a prefix in Taw, Tamar, Torridge and Teign. It was also chosen by Henry Williamson as the basis of Tarka in *Tarka the Otter*.

The Tarka Trail is a 180 mile (290km) trail for the walker (and, in part the cyclist as it uses a section of disused railway) following the South West Coast Path from Bideford to Lynton, then crossing Exmoor and heading south to Dartmoor (a short-cut variation heads west through West Buckland and Barnstaple). The Trail touches Dartmoor, following Belstone Cleave, going though Belstone and on to Okehampton from where it stays close to the River Torridge on its way to Bideford.

The Belstone Tor ridge seen from the north

HIGHEST DARTMOOR

MAPS:
Harvey Dartmoor North, OS Landranger Sheet 191, OS Outdoor Leisure Sheet 28 recommended

START/FINISH:
At 562917, the car park near the dam of Meldon Reservoir

No buses stop at Meldon Reservoir, or even on the main road close to the turn off for the reservoir. However, several DevonBuses stop at Sourton

DISTANCE/ASCENT:
11 miles (18km)/2,150ft (656m)

APPROXIMATE TIME:
6 hours

HIGHEST POINT:
High Willhays 2,038ft (621m)

REFRESHMENTS:
None on the route, but there is a 'Little Chef' on the A30 at the A386 junction (Sourton services) and plenty of choice in Okehampton

ADVICE:
A long, wild walk with sections of rough moor; visibility is often poor and a good map and compass skills are needed. However, there are some paths and the moor section has good landmarks

This walk lies within one of the Army's Dartmoor Firing Ranges. Please read the section on the ranges (pp.9–10) before setting out

Dartmoor's two highest peaks lie at the northern edge of the National Park, above Okehampton. This walk visits the pair of summits before continuing across wild moor and the West Okement River.

A   Meldon Reservoir

Some 20 years after Dartmoor became a National Park, the dam of Meldon Reservoir was completed and water from the West Okement River drowned the Meldon Gorge. It was also seen by many as drowning the principles behind the creation of National Parks in general and Dartmoor in particular.

That said, Meldon is a pleasant enough stretch of water, and does lie very close to the moor's edge – a reservoir at the heart of the moor would be a disaster: Dartmoor, for all its bogs, is a 'dry' landscape. Meldon's water is held in place by a dam 650ft (200m) long and 150ft (45m) high whose construction required almost 300,000 tons of concrete. The reservoir's water surface covers about 60 acres (25 ha).

a   From the car park entrance, turn left along the lane, following it to the reservoir dam. Cross the dam, go through the gate at the end and then immediately left through another gate to reach steps that descend to the dam base. Follow an indistinct path beside the West Okement River (which takes the reservoir spillage), crossing a tributary of the river (Red-a-ven Brook) (564920), which descends from the right, by

The calm serenity of Meldon Reservoir

stepping stones. To the left, soon after, is Meldon Pool, which although hidden from the track can be visited by making a detour across the West Okement River, using a footbridge (564921) which soon becomes visible.

The summit of Yes Tor

B   Meldon Pool

The pool is a flooded quarry from which limestone was extracted and burned in local kilns to produce agricultural lime. The walk passes close to a well-preserved kiln. The later quarry to the north-east of the pool was worked by British Rail to produce ballast for rail tracks. Originally wagons of ballast stone were hauled both north-east towards Okehampton, and over Meldon Viaduct, a magnificent iron bridge erected in 1874. The viaduct is 540ft (165m) long and up to 150ft (46m) high, and is a listed building, but it has not carried trains for many years.

The quarry to the east of the pool, and close to the route as it follows Red-a-ven Brook, was for the extraction of aplite, an even-grained, quartz-feldspar mineral used in the ceramics and glass industries. In the 1920s a bottle factory was built beside the quarry to make use of the aplite. The owners predicted it would be the biggest in the country, but they were wrong, the venture soon failing.

b   Continue north-east along the faint path to the next tributary, which flows through a stone building on the left that borders the track. Cross the side stream using stepping stones and turn right along a grass track, soon passing close to the aplite quarry. A well-defined stony track leaves the ruined quarry and disused bottle factory buildings, leading east then south-east beside the Red-a-ven which is to the right of the track. After about ¼ mile (400m), where the stony surfacing ceases, and the track curves left away from the brook at some old spoil heaps, fork right, cross a ford and remain on low ground in the flat-bottomed valley, still keeping the brook close on your right-hand side, and crossing the line of firing range notice boards denoting your entry into the military area of Okehampton Range (at approx 571913).

C   Red-a-ven Brook and Blackdown Mine

The stream is delightful, but should not be underestimated. On 17 August 1917 heavy rain caused it to increase its flow by an estimated 4,000-fold, the stream becoming a torrent which was able to shift boulders weighing several tons with ease. A temporary dam formed by an accumulation of boulders caused the Brook to expand to over 250ft (80m)

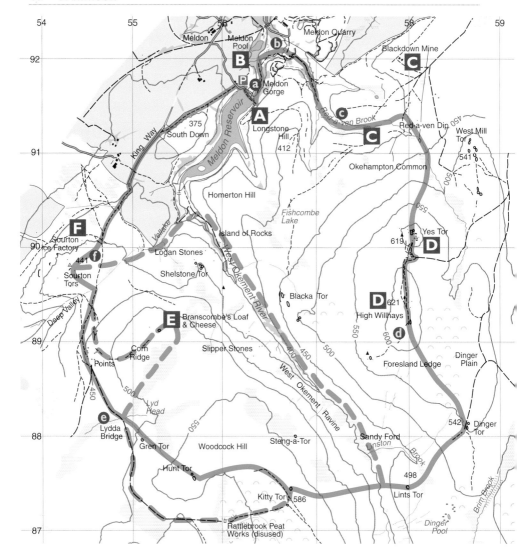

wide. Amazingly, at the time of Red-a-ven's evolution from chattering stream to awesome river, the nearby (and usually much larger) West Okement River carried no more than the usual 'heavy rain' flow. Fortunately, when the Red-a-ven rose there were no villages in its path.

Blackdown Mine was worked with great enthusiasm – and through a succession of names: it had been Devon Copper and Wheal Maria at earlier times – but little success.

c   Continue east for about another ¾ mile (1.2km) beside, or close to, Red-a-ven as it leaves the valley and climbs to reach a small pool (581911), once the reservoir for Okehampton. Here, cross Red-a-ven at any convenient spot and continue uphill (SE) to reach suitably dry ground before branching off right to climb Yes Tor (2,030ft/619m). From the summit (581901) head south to reach High Willhays (2,037ft/621m), Dartmoor's highest peak.

D   High Willhays and Yes Tor

Yes Tor is by far the most prominent of the two peaks and deserves to be the highest, but is actually 8ft (2.5m) lower than the fairly non-descript High Willhays. Yes Tor has a real tor, a trig point, a flagpole, and useful huts below the steep face for shelter. By contrast High Willhays has some large rocks. Some say Yes Tor is actually a corruption of 'ighest Tor (as the locals would say it), but this seems to be contradicted by the idea that Willhays derives from the Celtic 'ewhella', meaning 'highest'. Brown Willy, Bodmin Moor's highest peak, just a (relatively) short distance to the south-west is almost certainly a corruption of 'bryn ewhella', 'highest hill'. But High Willhays would then be a repetitive name, a fact that has led some to suggest that Willhays derives from 'gwylfa', Celtic for a look-out. If Yes Tor is not from 'ighest', it is likely to derive from East Tor, shortened to Eastor, then, because of the local dialect, heard as 'yeez tor'.

d   From High Willhays (580895) follow the grassy path towards the south-east to Dinger Tor, the knuckle-shaped tor ahead of you to the left. Be careful not to stray to the right of the path line as the ground can be very wet. A military road reaches the observation post on the tor and this can be used for the last section of the journey if you stray too far to the east.

From Dinger Tor head south-west, on grass (not the line of the path heading south to Dinger Pool), first descending to cross a brook, then climbing to the shapely Lints Tor (580875). Below the tor (W) is the West Okement River. Descend west to the river (at 576876); other possible crossing points are Sandy Ford to the north (574879), or Brim Ford by Kneeset Foot (579867) to the south. It is a difficult crossing, especially after rain.

If the river is impassable, there is a good route north-west to Sourton Tors following the east bank. Leave the Okehampton Range at 570885. The path passes Black-a-Tor Copse, one of

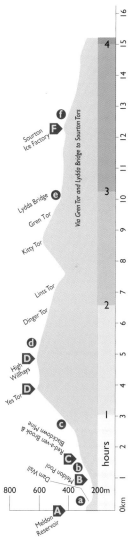

three surviving upland oak copses on Dartmoor (see note to Walk 5), and continues north-west to the footbridge over the West Okement at Vellake Corner (555906). Cross over, making for the north-south track, up a short bank to the west. Turn left (S) along the track, and then cross a lively stream, which is followed upwards (SW) through a small valley. Near the top the route joins King Way and proceeds west to Sourton Tors (543898).

If you are able to cross the West Okement, there is a short, rough, ascent of 550ft (170m) up the wet and uneven bank to Kitty Tor (567875), becoming less steep as you reach the broad moorland plateau topped by this tiny tor. Leave the Okehampton Range at 569875, in an area of rough, open moorland. Care is needed with navigation, especially in mist.

From Kitty Tor there are two routes, the first more suitable in dry conditions, which follows the remains of an old track north-west to the 1,873ft/571m trig. point, then west, and again north-west, passing Hunt Tor (557875) and Gren Tor, reaching the disused tramway at Lydda Bridge (549882). The second is stony, but drier and in better shape for poor weather. Head briefly south from Kitty Tor, then west to pick up a well-marked path west-south-west, joining the old tramway (559871). Follow this west, through a cutting, and veering north-west and then north, to cross the Lyd (549882).

E Branscombe's Loaf and Cheese
Legend has it that the Loaf is named from Walter Branscombe, a 13th century Bishop of Exeter whose diocese included almost all of Devon and Cornwall. One day, while travelling from Okehampton to Tavistock the bishop and his manservant became lost in a Dartmoor mist. They lost the track and finished here on Corn Ridge. Tired, nervous and hungry the pair stopped and the bishop is said to have called out that he would give anything for something to eat. At that moment a man appeared out of the mist and offered the pair bread and cheese. As the bishop was about to take it, his servant caught a glimpse of cloven hoof below the man's cloak – it was the Devil in disguise. The servant shouted a warning and the bishop dropped the bread and cheese which instantly turned to rocks. It is a good story, but experts claim more mundane reasons for the name. The name 'loaf' is though to be from the Celtic 'llof', a lump (or rock), while Branscombe could be from the Celtic 'bran cwm', 'raven valley'. It has been pointed out that the Celts would have said 'cwm bran' (as with the town of that name in South Wales), but later folk, more

Prewley Moor with West Mill Tor and Yes Tor in the distance

used to 'combe' following, rather than preceding, a name could easily have changed the order. The 'cheese' is, of course, just an outcrop smaller than the 'loaf'.

e From Lydda Bridge, a longer and harder, but enjoyable way, adding about 1 mile (1.3km) and 164ft (50m) ascent, is to proceed north-north-west over rough ground – small paths appear in the light vegetation – to Corn Ridge and Branscombe's Loaf (553891), descending south-west and later north by a track shown on the map, from the south-west end of Corn Ridge to meet King Way (545893), an old route linking Tavistock and Okehampton. In dry conditions a direct, but steepish, descent can, instead, be made north-west.

The summit of High Willhays. Yes Tor can be seen behind the walker

The shorter way from Lydda bridge continues along the old tramway north-north-west and north, passing the sharp-angled turning where the tramway changed direction, and joining the King Way (545893), at a shallow col, then bearing off to the left (NW) for the spectacular top of Sourton Tors (543898). Close to the top is an area of hummocky ground which has so far defied geological interpretation.

F   Sourton Ice Factory
During the 19th century shallow troughs were dug in the moor close to a spring near the top of Sourton Tors. During the winter spring water was diverted into the troughs where, overnight, it froze. The following morning the ice would be collected and transported by horse-drawn cart to the railway at Meldon. There it would be transferred by train to Plymouth where fishermen would collect it to preserve their catches. Sadly the long transportation to Plymouth allowed most of the ice to thaw and the factory soon ceased production.

f From Sourton Tors, head north-east past the remains of the Sourton Ice Factory; the big grey building away to the left is the Prewley Water Treatment Plant. Maintain direction to meet a long stone wall to your right, which we now follow for some way, passing a tall granite gatepost until another wall (left) closes in, and we reach a gateway (550907), close to where the two walls meet, in the corner. Go through the gate and follow the wall-enclosed track beyond. When the wall on the right ends, go through the gate and bear right at the footpath finger post to Meldon Reservoir; do not go through the next gate ahead. Follow the path sign at the corner of the wall, turning left, and continuing along the north side of South Down, with the wall on your left, to reach the road opposite the car park entrance.

POSTBRIDGE AND CRANMERE POOL

MAPS:
Harvey Dartmoor North, OS
Landranger Sheets 191, OS
Outdoor Leisure Sheet 28

START/FINISH:
There are two car parks at
Postbridge, one at the National
Park Centre (at 647788) on the
north side of the B3212 and
one on south side, further
away from the road bridge, at
646787. Postbridge is served
by DevonBuses 82 and 98

DISTANCE/ASCENT:
16¼ miles (26km)/1,200ft
(360m)

APPROXIMATE TIME:
7 hours

HIGHEST POINT:
Hangingstone Hill and Cut Hill,
1,978ft (603m)

REFRESHMENTS:
Inns at Postbridge and Two
Bridges

ADVICE:
This is a long and arduous
outing, by far the hardest in
the book and should only be
attempted by experienced
walkers with good equipment
and absolute assuredness with
map and compass

This walk lies within two of
the Army's Dartmoor Firing
Ranges. Please read the
Section on the ranges (see
pp.9–10) before setting out

Cranmere Pool is the most sought-after of Dartmoor's features and letterboxes. Once it was the moor's most inaccessible point, but the military road which heads south from the Okehampton camp, has made it much easier to reach. This route visits the Pool from Postbridge, making a long tour of the northern moor and visiting the present 'point of inaccessibility' – Fur Tor.

A Postbridge

There have been farms in the Postbridge area for many years, but the hamlet only grew up in the 18th century as a stopping place on the turnpike road from Moretonhampstead to Tavistock and the centre for a couple of enterprises for which Dartmoor seems a most unlikely centre. The Hullet brothers grew potatoes on a stretch of moorland and extracted starch from them in a factory at the hamlet. The starch factory was never very successful and was subsequently used as a sheep fold, the brothers doing rather better when they built the hamlet's first inn. Equally strange, a gunpowder factory was built on the moor to the south-west of Postbridge. The remnants of this powder mill, with its chimneys and an old mortar used for firing a standard cannonball – the distance the ball was thrown was measured to check on powder quality. The B3212 is said to be haunted by a hairy-handed beast. Some say the beast is a dog, but others claim the hands are human, though covered in coarse black hair. Only the hands are seen, usually scratching at the windows of parked cars or caravans, or tearing at the fabric of a tent, but occasionally appearing at very close quarters, to the horror of the viewer. Drivers and cyclists on the B3212 near Postbridge have also reported invisible hands grasping their steering wheels or handle bars and attempting to steer them off the road.

On a much less harrowing note, Postbridge is also the site of one of Dartmoor's most famous and picturesque clapper bridges. Clapper bridges are slabs of stone laid across streams. In its simplest form the clapper is a single slab laid bank-to-bank. Wider rivers required several slabs, pillars supporting the slab ends. If the rivers were also prone to flooding, the pillars were tall, taking the slabs above the expected flood level. At Postbridge the granite slabs have

been used to give a span of 43ft (13m), and the pillars are the tallest of any Dartmoor clapper, the East Dart River being prone to severe flooding. The pillars are also shaped on the upstream side so as to shed the applied force of a rush of water and, hopefully, avoid the collapse of the bridge. Many of Dartmoor's clappers have been torn down by flooding of rivers, but it is said that one stone of the Postbridge clapper was dismantled in an abortive attempt to prevent a family of ducks swimming down stream and so out of range of their cooking pots. The original river crossing in Postbridge was the stepping stones which lie about 110 yards (100m) upstream from the road bridge. In the past it was thought by some that clapper bridges may be prehistoric in origin, and some books still claim that the Dartmoor clappers date from the time of the moor's megalithic monuments. While it is almost certainly true that folk skilled enough to move and raise the stones of the moor's stone circles would have created simple bridges, there is no evidence that any of the clappers pre-date the medieval period when they were constructed as packhorse bridges. The Postbridge clapper is likely to be even younger, dating from the time of local tin mining. Close to the bridge is a mould stone into which molten tin was poured to produce ingots which were then taken by packhorse to Chagford.

The clapper bridge at Postbridge is the largest on the moor

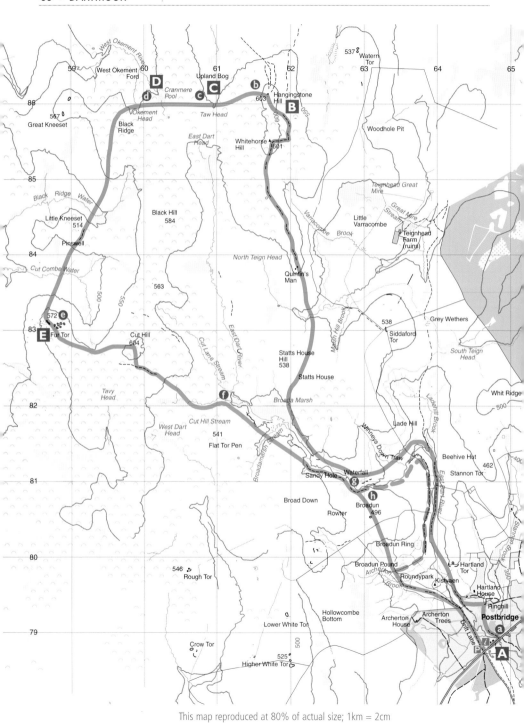

This map reproduced at 80% of actual size; 1km = 2cm

To the north-east of the clapper, beside the B3212, is Postbridge's church, built in 1867 and dedicated to St Gabriel. In its time the church has also served as the hamlet's school and meeting room.

a   From Postbridge (see Walk 7 para a) cross the road bridge over the East Dart, eastward, and after a few yards go left through a gate to the footpath heading north for Ringhill Farm. The path turns left towards the river just before the farm, and continues north-west along the river bank, passing Hartland Farm (right). The way continues on the flank of Hartland Tor and moves to a higher level because of boggy areas. After passing under Stannon Tor the path crosses Ladehill Brook (639813).

From here the Beehive hut (640814) is just to the north, but our path climbs south-west through a wall gate (636814), keeping well above the East Dart, and finally contours towards the picturesque waterfall at 627811. Continue north-west through Sandy Hole Pass (see Note to Walk 7), and look for a path to the right (north and not easy to find), soon leaving the river and rounding the east side of Broad Marsh (619818) where the path becomes indistinct. From here head north to Marsh Hill Pass (619823) (Statts House Cut), where a clear path follows the shallow and ill-defined peat pass. Both ends are marked by a short granite post and plaque. Statts House (see Note to Walk 7) lies to the south-east and Statts House Hill (OS Winney's Down) is north-west (621826). Enter the Okehampton Range at 620830.

From Statts House Hill the way descends gently to the North Teign River, and then follows range poles to the summit of Quintin's Man (621838), with its hut and range flagpoles. From Quintin's Man a track heads west of north to Whitehorse Hill (617861). Bear right (E) through the Whitehorse Pass, an early peat pass widened (by bulldozer) in 1963, then turn left (N) across the flank of Hangingstone Hill. The direct route to the summit is very boggy and so it is best to go along the hill's east flank until firmer ground allows a direct route to the top.

B   Hangingstone Hill

Benjamin Gayer was a Mayor of Okehampton in the 17th century, but this respectability was a shield for his activities as a sheep stealer. Eventually Gayer was caught and, after his trial, sentenced to death. The execution may have been carried out here, and it is certain that the ex-Mayor's body was gibbeted on the hill as an example to others. Legend has

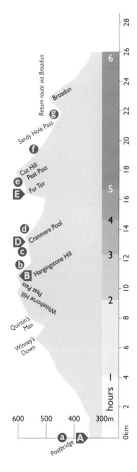

Please note: time taken calculated according to the Naismith Formula (see p.2)

it that Gayer's spirit was also punished, being required to empty Cranmere Pool with a sieve.

b A path heads west from the observation post on the summit, but is soon lost in the bogs near Taw Head.

C Upland Bog

Granite is an impervious rock, the high, but shallow sloping, moorland plateau therefore draining poorly. The hard, erosion-resistant rock also produces a poor, acidic soil which supports a limited range of plants. The soil is often waterlogged and when plants die their decay is inhibited by lack of oxygen and bacteria, the latter kept at bay by acids leached from the rock and soil. The result of only partial decay is the creation of a brown, mud-like moss-peat. On the hillsides the peat forms the basis of upland (or blanket) bog, while in the valleys it lies below the valley bogs (or mires). Upland bog is the sponge that feeds Dartmoor's rivers, but the peaty base occasionally dries, shrinking and cracking to form peat hags which are as difficult to traverse as the bogs themselves. The bogs are home to bog cotton, rushes, sedges and mosses, particularly sphagnum moss. There are also rarer plants such as the insectivorous sundew and butterwort, and the very rare bog orchid. The drier sections of the peat moss support ling, crowberry (which is at the southern limit of its range), whortleberry and flowers such as tormentil. Upland bog is home to the golden plover and dunlin, while the drier sections of bog (upland heath) support red grouse, skylarks, wheatear, stonechat and ring ouzels.

c From Taw Head there is an indefinite path across the bogs to Cranmere Pool (at 603858), which lies almost due west of Hangingstone Hill.

Black Ridge Peat Pass and plaque

D Cranmere Pool

Some say that Cranmere is the crow pool, named for the ravens which frequent the area, others that it is crane pool, named for the herons which fished it in its prime. Today ravens are still seen, though the herons have long gone. Although moormen had visited Cranmere for centuries, the first recorded 'tourist' trip was made by John Andrews, a Devonian lawyer, who walked to the pool in 1789. In the next century trips to wilderness areas became the vogue among the leisured classes and Cranmere became a popular destination, with local folk acting as guides. In 1854 one of the guides, James Perrott, built a cairn at the pool, inside which he placed a glass jar into which his clients could drop their visiting cards, and a visitors' book which they could sign. At around the same time the peat wall which held back the pool was breached, whether by storm or by human hand has never been established. If by hand, what the motive might have been is equally unclear: one story is that a local shepherd breached the peat well after several of his sheep drowned in the pool. However, it is also worth noting that some experts wonder whether there ever was a real pool rather than shallow ponds among the peat hags, so that there never was a wall to breach. The pool drained away and Cranmere became the marshy area we now see. In periods of dry weather the pool all but disappears, but in very wet periods a shallow pool (or, correctly, a series of small pools) is re-established.

Cranmere Pool letterbox

d To the west of Cranmere Pool, which stands at about 1,836ft (560m), there are two vague hills, Black Ridge and tor-topped Great Kneeset. Aim for the latter to reach the northern end of the Black Ridge peat pass (598859), another cut by Frank Phillpotts (see Walk 7), its entrance marked by a memorial stone to him. Follow the pass south over Black Ridge (to 595849) then head for the obvious tor on Fur Tor, crossing Black Ridge Water and descending to another Peat Pass, Pinswell Pass, to the east of Little Kneeset, which aids descent to Cut Combe Water if a direct route is favoured. A ford across Black Ridge Water links these two passes. Alternatively contour around the head of Cut Combe Water valley before ascending Fur Tor (588831).

E Fur Tor

Exact calculations may suggest another spot, but for most Dartmoor walkers Fur Tor is the 'point of inaccessibility', the furthest point of the moor from any road. It is a marvellous place, its summit topped by huge granite blocks – a real tor.

Fur Tor

Not surprisingly its letterbox is one of the moor's most sought-after, and its huge rock pile and remoteness have persuaded followers of Earth Magic that it is a supernatural place, a focus point for natural forces. The moormen have long claimed that the tor (to them it was the 'Vur Tor', the far tor, another indication of its remoteness) was the home of the fairy folk and within living memory walkers claimed to have seen a pixie sitting on the top.

e   Head south-east from the summit of Fur Tor, on good paths veering left to contour round the valley head of Cut Combe Water (593827), and crossing here from the Okehampton Range to the Merrivale Range. Go east following the curve of the plateau to the flattish top of Cut Hill (598828, 1,978ft/603m).

From the summit of Cut Hill, go south towards the TV mast on North Hessary Tor, to intersect the line of the 'North West Passage' which avoids a wild hillside of peat hags, and is followed east-south-east through the peat pass. Continue in the same general direction on a path soon lost in the difficult wilderness (heading for two range boards), down the slight valley which follows. Continue south-east to reach Cut Hill Stream (unnamed on OS map which gives that name to Cut Lane Stream) and head east, crossing to the south bank when possible, before the marsh area near its confluence with the East Dart, and continuing towards the East Dart. Leave the Merrivale Range at 607820.

f On reaching the East Dart, turn south-east and follow small tracks, away from but parallel to the river; Broad Marsh lies opposite. Cross Broad Marsh Stream (619817) between conspicuous rock-topped hillocks, continuing to Sandy Hole Pass (619818). Follow the riverside through the pass until a wider valley is reached, where the rivers veers east and the upper path is easier. A leat may be noticed opposite (625812); shortly after, the hillside becomes rockier, and just around the bend you pass the waterfall seen on the outward route (627811).

g From the waterfall, continue south-east over the hillside and down to a side valley (629809), where the river turns east and the paths divide. Go ahead (E) over the hillside for the riverside route, continuing until the river bends north-west and the hillside becomes rocky, where the path rejoins the riverside crossing a stile in a wall (637813), before rounding the bend opposite Beehive. From here the path by the leat heads south-west to Braddon Lake.

h For the shorter route, much of the way heads south-south-west, first bearing right up the hillside of Broadun 1,617ft (496m), east of Broad Down, with its flat-topped rocks, then gently down to a wall immediately below. Cross the stile and maintain direction. Both routes cross to Braddon Lake (clapper bridge), to reach Drift Lane near the East Dart (643794) and Postbridge.

Looking north-west from Hangingstone Hill

VIXEN TOR

MAPS:
Harvey Dartmoor South, OS
Landranger Sheet 191, OS
Outdoor Leisure Sheet 28

START/FINISH:
There are several car parks beside the B3357 between Merrivale and the top of Park Hill which drops down into Tavistock. The best one for this walk is that at 531751 at the top of the hill. From it there are fine views towards Tavistock and the western edge of the National Park

DevonBuses 98 (Bellever to Tavistock), 98A (Plymouth to Tavistock via Princetown) and 172 (Totnes to Tavistock) all stop at Merrivale, to the east of the route

DISTANCE/ASCENT:
3¾ miles (6km)/200ft (60m)

APPROXIMATE TIME:
1½ hours

HIGHEST POINT:
Vixen Tor 1,040ft (317m)

REFRESHMENTS:
The Dartmoor Inn, Merrivale is 1½ miles (2.5km) to the east and in summer there are usually ice-cream and tea/coffee/sandwich vans in the car park

ADVICE:
A fine walk with little climbing. Care must be taken to avoid Vixana's bog

A delightful short walk to a distinctive tor associated with one of Dartmoor's best witch legends.

Looking towards Pew Tor from Feather Tor

a From the western end of the car park – where there is a panorama dial pointing out the various features of the superb westward view – head south, soon reaching (and following) a track edged by large boulders. Follow the track across a leat, with shallow Barn Hill off to the left, and on to a wall elbow on the right. Continue for another 200 yards (183m) to reach another wall elbow and there turn sharp left east along a faint path to reach an old cross beside a leat (534743).

A   Windy Post
The waterway is the Grimstone and Sortridge Leat, noted on Walk 4. The leat was constructed in medieval times, perhaps as many as 500 years ago, and provided water for farmers, tin miners and, later, quarrymen. The cross, known as Windy Post or, occasionally, as Beckamoor Cross, is also thought to be medieval, marking the junction of ancient tracks that linked Tavistock to Chagford and Ashburton. As the cross also stood on the moorland plateau it was probably erected not only to mark the track junction, but as a 'Thank God' cross, marking the top of the stiff climb on to the moor from Tavistock.

Very close to the cross, in the leat channel, there is a bullseye stone. These disc-like stones with a small hole drilled through them were used to control the amount of water which was drained from a main channel into a side channel. Such side channels would have taken water to a farm and discussions would agree the quantity of water which could be taken and, therefore, the size of the bullseye. Disputes over water, with unscrupulous farmers taking more than their share, or blocking supplies to others, seem to have occurred a few times.

b From Windy Post, climb Feather Tor ahead south-east and bear right through the summit clitter of boulders, crossing open moor beside another leat to reach Pu Tor (mislabelled as Pew Tor – 531736 – on OS Maps), with its fine collection of tors and boulders. From the summit, head due east to reach a wall and turn left to follow the track beside it, walking north-north-east with the wall on your right and, soon, Heckwood Tor on your left. At the old Heckwood granite quarry the large dressed block was formed to be part of the Plymouth breakwater which was constructed in 1812. The block was discovered to be flawed and abandoned.

Windy Post beside the Grimstone and Sortridge Leat

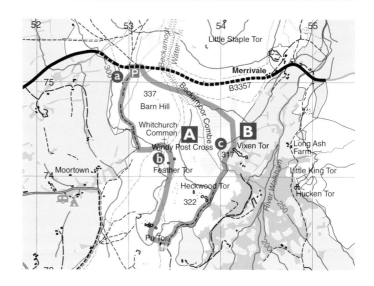

The track descends to Beckamoor Water (540741) which is crossed to reach a stile over the wall ahead. Take care as there can be deep boggy ground on both sides of the stream and on both sides of the ford. Beyond the stile is Vixen Tor (542742).

B   Vixen Tor

The massive lump that is Vixen Tor lies on private land outside the access land area of the moor. Access is allowed by way of the stiles in the boundary wall to the west of the tor, but please remember that you are on private land and act accordingly. Dogs are not allowed on this private land. The tor is one of the best on Dartmoor for rock climbers, perhaps bettered only by Haytor/Low Man. All the routes to the top are at the top end of the difficulty range, so walkers with little experience and no equipment should be very cautious.

The strange rock shapes of Vixen Tor

Vixen Tor is almost certainly named for a regularly used fox lair, but has come to be recognised as the ancient home of the witch Vixana, although her legend seems to have been a little vague as to the actual spot, referring only to an outcrop between Two Bridges and Tavistock.

Vixana lived on top the tor, feeding on the bodies of those who were sucked down by the bog that lay between it and Windy Post. The bog is still there, and can still cause the unwary grief, but in Vixana's day it was far worse, the witch having cast a spell over it so that it actively conspired to kill those trapped in it in exchange for a share of their bodies. Vixana's greatest trick was her ability to conjure mists. She would wait until a traveller reached Windy Post, then produce a mist which rapidly enveloped and disorientated him. As the traveller ploughed on, desperately looking for the path, the bog would open and devour him, the last noise he heard being the hideous cackle of Vixana's laughter as she anticipated her next meal.

But one day Vixana met her match when the traveller was a man who had once helped a pixie trapped in a bog in another part of the moor. In gratitude the pixie had given the man a ring which allowed him to see through the moor's mists. He would also become invisible if he twisted the ring on his finger. As the man advanced eastwards from Windy Post Vixana summoned up a thick mist and licked her lips in anticipation. But the man could see clearly through the mist and accurately followed the path around the bog's southern edge. As he neared Vixen Tor the man heard Vixana's terrible cackle. He turned the ring and became invisible, and climbed the tor to see the source of the noise. Seeing Vixana he rapidly realised the truth and, rushing forward, hurled the witch off the tor. One version of the legend has it that the falling witch dislodged numerous boulders and was buried by them, the place of her entombment being the boulder-filled gully on the tor's northern side. But a much more poetic end to the tale suggests Vixana was consumed by the bog she had created.

c   There is another stile over the wall on the northern side of Vixen Tor. Cross this to regain open moor. Now head north-west across the moor, soon reaching Beckamoor Water, to your left. Follow the stream to reach an aqueduct taking the Grimstone and Sortridge Leat over the stream. Here, bear half-left, crossing the flank of Barn Hill to return to the car park.

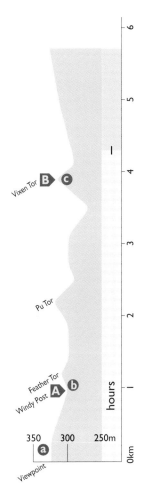

Please note: time taken calculated according to the Naismith Formula (see p.2)

MERRIVALE

MAPS:
Harvey Dartmoor South, OS
Landranger Sheet 191, OS
Outdoor Leisure Sheet 28

START/FINISH:
At 561749, the Four Winds car
park on the southern side of
the B3357 about 3 miles (5km)
west of Two Bridges

DevonBuses 98 (Bellever to
Tavistock), 98A (Plymouth to
Tavistock via Princetown) and
172 (Totnes to Tavistock) all
stop at Merrivale, to the west
of the route

DISTANCE/ASCENT:
4 miles (6.5km)/300ft (92m)

APPROXIMATE TIME:
1¾ hours

HIGHEST POINT:
1,246ft (380m) at Swelltor
Quarry

REFRESHMENTS:
There are inns at Two Bridges,
to the east, and Merrivale, to
the west, and several
possibilities at Princetown, to
the south-east

ADVICE:
The moorland section of the
walk can be boggy, but the
track around the quarries
offers good walking. The
quarries have several steep
walls: these offer long falls and
nasty landings to the unwary

This walk visits the most accessible, and one of the finest, prehistoric sites on the moor, then continues to a quarry site associated with the moor's most famous feature, the prison at Princetown.

a From the car park head south-west, then west across the moor following a leat to reach the megalithic sites (556748).

A   Merrivale Megaliths

The megaliths consist of three stone rows, several cairn circles and kistvaens, standing stones and some hut circles. The northern, double stone, row is 200 yards (180m) long and has a large standing stone – known as a blocking stone – at its eastern end. The southern row, also a double row, is almost 300 yards (about 265m) long and is also closed at its eastern end by a blocking stone. The two rows are not parallel, and though they are approximately east-west, neither aligns with a significant sunrise or sunset. They do, however, align with the May rise of Pleiades, a group of stars which the Greeks are known to have used to predict the time for harvesting. The Australian Aborigines also believed Pleiades to be a deeply significant stellar group. It has been shown that the slight difference in alignment of the two rows (they are about 2° from parallel) is consistent with the southern row being erected 200 years after the northern if the two are both aligned to Pleiades. But did an agrarian society really need a rising star group to tell them when their crops were ripe?

Almost exactly half way along the southern row (half-way to within 10ft/3m) is a cairn circle, a stone circle surrounding a cairn over a cremation site. The circle is hardly pronounced now, but most experts believe it did exist, and its presence makes the Merrivale row unique. A short distance south-west of the cairn circle is an excellent kistvaen (a burial 'box' for cremated remains formed from slabs of stone). There is another cairn a little further west and from it the third (indistinct) row heads south-west.

To the south of the rows there is another stone circle and several single standing stones, and heading south-east from close to the eastern end of the stone rows is a row of cairns

laid out in a straight line. Close to the cairns are the remains of several hut circles (see Note to Walk 7), an unusual feature as it is more normal for such (assumed) ritual sites to be set away from habitation. Perhaps the huts were for priests or a shaman. Excavations at the hut circles have not revealed objects which allow a dating of the site, but from the similarity with other sites it is likely that the Merrivale features are at least 4,000 years old.

Prehistoric stone rows (with 19th century leat between them) at Merrivale

Perhaps because the megaliths were so well known, this part of the moor was used as a 'Plague Market' during the time of the Black Death. Food grown on the moor was left here by the farmers and collected by folk from the towns at the moor's western edge. The townsfolk left cash at the site which was collected later by the farmer, neither group having to come into contact with the other. The quarantine worked, the moor folk escaping the plague relatively unscathed.

b   From the eastern (car park) end of the stone rows, head south-east following the row of cairns, then continuing across open moor to reach a large inscribed standing stone (557746).

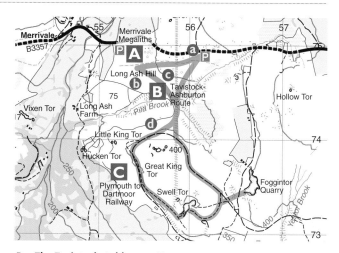

B   The Tavistock-Ashburton Route

The standing stone is inscribed 'T' on one side and 'A' on the other and is several thousand years newer than the Merrivale menhirs. In 1696 Parliament passed an Act compelling the major towns at the moor's edge to erect waymark stones to help travellers crossing the moor keep to better known tracks in poor weather. This is one such stone (there is another close by), the letters standing for Tavistock and Ashburton as it stood on the route between the two. When the first roads were built across the moor some of the old tracks were made redundant and many of the waymarkers were used as gateposts. The stones here are rare survivors.

c   Continue south-east, heading for the wall elbow ahead. Cross the Long Ash Brook as you reach the wall (558744) and follow it south (the wall is on your right) until it turns sharply right (W). Here go gently uphill south-west to reach the old trackbed of the Plymouth to Dartmoor Railway.

Abandoned granite corbels at Swell Tor Quarry

C Plymouth to Dartmoor Railway (the P and DR)

The railway was built by Thomas Tyrwhitt, an Essex man who became a friend of the Prince of Wales when the two were at Oxford University. In 1786 the friendship led to Tyrwhitt's appointment as auditor for the Duchy of Cornwall. On his way to take up the post Tyrwhitt passed Dartmoor and decided that what it needed was a town at its heart peopled by folk who would tame the wilderness and make him rich. He therefore organised the building of the town, calling it Prince's Town after his patron. Those who were moved into it soon shortened the name to Princetown, but equally quickly found that the moor would not be tamed.

The future for Tyrwhitt's town looked bleak, but this was the time of the Napoleonic Wars and Tyrwhitt noted the rising public disquiet about the conditions of the French prisoners of war in the prison hulks at Plymouth. He proposed the building of a prison at his new town and soon French, and some American prisoners from the War of Independence, were toiling on the construction of Dartmoor's famous, and famously bleak, prison. The weather, the local geography and difficulties of transport caused seemingly endless delays, but finally, in 1809, the first prisoners were moved in: the prison has been in use practically ever since.

After his efforts with the prison Tyrwhitt was made Sir Thomas and appointed Black Rod, but his interest in Dartmoor, and specifically the area around Princetown, continued. He next decided that what was needed was a railway which would import lime to 'sweeten' the acidic moorland soil, coal to heat the houses of Princetown, food and timber, and would export Dartmoor granite, peat and the hemp and flax which would be grown on the moor. The scheme would 'clothe with grain and grasses a spacious tract of land now lying barren, desolate and neglected ... and fill this unoccupied region with an industrious and hardly population ... (and) create a profitable interchange of useful commodities'. To pursue this worthy aim Tyrwhitt began the construction of the railway and began selling the granite which would be carried along it. One of his earliest contracts was to supply granite for London Bridge. But his railway, partially granite-sleepered and, initially, horse-drawn, took much longer than planned to complete. It was to have been double-tracked, but was reduced to a single track to save time. Even so, the London Bridge contract was lost to Aberdeen (and Haytor) granite, causing Tyrwhitt to furiously complain of a gross injustice which implied that his stone was

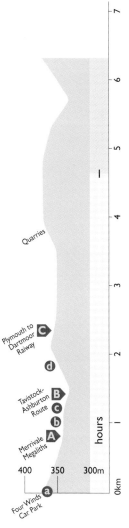

Please note: time taken calculated according to the Naismith Formula (see p.2)

inferior to that from Scottish or other Dartmoor quarries. The railway was completed in 1827. Later it was steam-hauled and became part of GWR, but it was never really profitable and finally closed in 1956.

d Turn right, west, along the old trackbed, following it around Great King Tor (OS King's Tor). Follow the track over a lovely granite bridge with a superb view into the Walkham Valley to the west. At a track fork the right branch heads off towards Plymouth: take the left branch which served the Swell Tor Quarry. To the side of this track are some beautifully tooled corbels, part of a consignment for London Bridge, dumped after the contract was lost. The trackbed also has some old wooden sleepers, now well rotted and with protruding rusty iron bolts – please take care.

At a ruined building, on the right, a trackbed goes off left through a narrow, rocky gorge, soon reaching an atmospheric quarry pit, now water-filled. Continue along the main trackbed, bearing left at a fork, then right at the next one, and

descending to reach a raised causeway through another quarry. To the right a moss-hung face drips water into a black pool.

The track now bears left and becomes less distinct, but a more distinct track can be seen to the right. This was the line from Princetown, the two tracks joining a little way ahead (at 563734). At the junction a short detour north-eastwards visits the Foggintor Quarry which has a larger water-filled pit and the remnants of some old machinery, including a granite lifting crane. The quarry edge is vertical so care is required e.g. in fog or slippery conditions.

Our route continues north-westward between Swell Tor, left, and Foggin Tor, right, crossing the moor and then rounding Great King Tor to regain the point at which the trackbed was reached. Now reverse the outward route to the furthest wall elbow and then head north-east across open, and boggy, moorland to regain the start.

Foggintor Quarry in the grip of winter

HAYTOR

To the east of Widecombe-in-the-Moor, the high moorland plateau falls into the Bovey Valley. The last section of high land in this area is topped by one of the most accessible of Dartmoor's tors. Haytor is a compact mass of stone, imposing rather than picturesque. From it there are fine views of the South Devon coast and an equally fine walk around an old quarry site.

MAPS:
Harvey Dartmoor North, OS Landranger Sheet 191, OS Outdoor Leisure Sheet 28

START/FINISH:
At 759767, the car park on the southern side of the B3387 linking Bovey Tracey to Widecombe-in-the-Moor

DevonBuses 170 and 171, both of which take circular routes from Newton Abbot, stopping at Buckfast Abbey and Widecombe, stop at the Moorland Hotel, Haytor. The buses run only on Sundays and Public Holidays

DISTANCE/ASCENT:
3 miles (5km)/600ft (180m)

APPROXIMATE TIME:
1½ hours

HIGHEST POINT:
Haytor, 1,499ft (457m)

REFRESHMENTS:
In summer there is usually an ice cream or drinks/snacks van in the car park. There are inns at Widecombe, 3 miles (5km) to the west, and in Haytor Vale, the village a mile or so to the east, off the B3387

ADVICE:
The walk to Haytor is very easy, but the moorland section of the walk is rougher, though never remote, the tor acting as a permanent waymarker unless visibility is very poor

The first part of the walk follows this broad grassy track to Haytor

a   From the car park, cross the road and follow the broad grassy swathe north to Haytor.

A   Haytor (note: Hey Tor on Harvey map)

The tor's name is occasionally spelled 'hey', but as hay or hey is only a rendering of the local pronunciation of 'high' it matters little. The main tor is a vast, compact mass of rock with uncompromising west and north faces, but straightforward ascents on the other sides. Walkers accompanied by children should be careful: the steep faces are totally unguarded and a fall down either is likely to be fatal.

Rock climbing on the western face of Haytor

Low Man, the second 'tor', is a quite different feature. Technically this is not a tor at all, being an exposed section of rock set in the hillside. It is tall and steep – again be careful if approaching the top edge – and plastered with rock climbs at the middling order of difficulty. By personal preference (and almost common ascent) Interrogation (E3, 150ft, 6a, 5b), up the centre of the highest part of the wall, is the best rock climb on the Dartmoor tors.

b   Walk past the rock mass, on your right, and pause. Down and right (NE) you will see the remains of Haytor Quarry. Follow the rough track to it. A track takes you north through the quarry, which is fenced. The old quarry has a small lake and interesting flora.

B   Haytor Quarry

In 1792 James Templer, a local entrepreneur, was given permission to dig a canal from Bovey Tracey to the River Teign at Stover. The canal was completed in 1794 and made the Templers enough money for James' son, George, to open quarries near Haytor, transporting the stone to Bovey Tracey for onward shipment by canal barge and ship from Teignmouth. To transport the stone from the quarries Templer eventually built a tramway, though this did not open until 1820. The tramway used granite rails rather than iron – granite was readily available, and lasted longer than iron – and had the flanges on the rails rather than on the carriage wheels as was more usually the case. The problem with granite rails was the creation of curves. To produce them the rails were packed up with stone, the carriage wheels then wearing a correct rebate and angle with continuous usage.

The stone from Templer's quarries – Haytor, Holwell Tor and the wholly inappropriately named Rubble Heap – was first

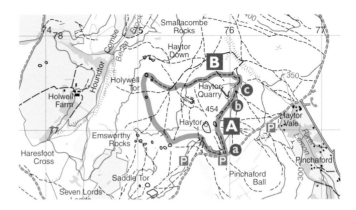

class and used on several prestigious projects. Most significantly it was used for the arches of London Bridge, to the aggravation of Sir Thomas Tyrwhitt, owner of the Swell Tor/Foggin Tor quarries (see Note to Walk 12). Haytor stone was also used for the columns of the old British Library.

Initially the stone was cut into blocks by scoring a line along the proposed edging and then cutting a groove with chisels. When the groove was deep enough wedges were placed at intervals along it and pounded into the block until it split. This was time-consuming and hard work and was eventually

Haytor Quarry

replaced by the tare and feather method. Here a series of holes about 3in (7.6cm) deep would be excavated at intervals (usually every 6in/15.2cm) along the proposed edge. Into the holes a pair of curved metal feathers would be inserted. The wedge-shaped tare would then be inserted between the feathers. The line of tares would then be bashed in turn until the block split. Tare and feather was quicker than groove and wedge, but still required awesome hard work by men with arms like Popeye. Occasionally the block did not split even when the tares were fully inserted. Further holes between the tares would then be excavated, though occasionally the block would be abandoned, a search of the old quarries sometimes revealing a block with tares and feathers still in situ.

After the blocks of stone had been created they were put on flat-bed carriages and horse-drawn along the granite tramway to Bovey Tracey for barge shipment to Teignmouth and reloading on to ships. But granite is heavy and the triple loading/unloading was time-consuming and expensive. Eventually, good though the Haytor stone was, it became uncompetitive and the quarries ceased operation in 1858.

Today the Haytor quarries, the largest Templer quarries, are fenced off – though gates allow access – as they are water-filled and dangerous. But they are also havens for wildlife, trees and shrubs growing in the sheltered pits and dragon- and damselflies breeding in the ponds. The water is acidic and so supports a limited range of plants: look out for the yellow, heart-shaped flowers of shoreweed. Of the dragonflies the most likely to be seen are the common and southern hawkers, large dragonflies with vivid green and blue spotted bodies, and the black darter.

c From the gate in the fence surrounding the largest quarry head north-east to reach a Y-junction of tracks (761775). Turn left (NNW) here, following the Templer Way, the old granite tramway route, to its junction with the main tramway. Turn left along the old track, going through a cutting and then heading across the moor to the old quarry at Holwell Tor.

After exploring the quarry and enjoying the view of Haytor, head south-east towards the latter, crossing the line of the tramway which served the Rubble Heap Quarry. There is no path, but Haytor is a beacon ahead as you cross the bilberry-covered moorland.

From Haytor reverse the outward route back to the start.

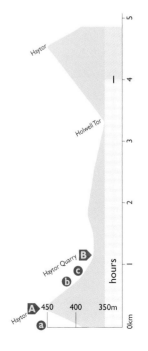

Please note: time taken calculated according to the Naismith Formula (see p.2)

FOALE'S ARRISHES

This short walk from a well-known viewpoint is a good introduction to Dartmoor as it includes open moor, two good tors, prehistoric remains and a geological curiosity.

MAPS:
Harvey Dartmoor North, OS Landranger Sheet 191, OS Outdoor Leisure Sheet 28

START/FINISH:
At 735767, the car park on the northern side of the B3387 at the high point of the road between Haytor and Widecombe. There is another car park on the other side of the road a little further on

DevonBuses 170 and 171, both of which take circular routes from Newton Abbot, stopping at Buckfast Abbey, stop at the Moorland Hotel, Haytor and at Widecombe. The buses run only on Sundays and Public Holidays

DISTANCE/ASCENT:
2½ miles (3.5km)/475ft (145m)

APPROXIMATE TIME:
1½ hours

REFRESHMENTS:
None on the route, but several possibilities in Widecombe which is just 1¼ miles (2km) to the west

ADVICE:
Relatively easy walking and route finding unless the weather is very poor; part of the walk can be boggy and also goes through bracken and gorse

a From the car park head east of south uphill to the summit of Top Tor, on the southern side of the road. From the tor there is a fine view, slightly better than the well-known one from the car park, the effort of climbing 100ft (30m) being well rewarded. To the north are Bonehill Rocks, while north-west is the long ridge of Hamel Down beyond the East Webburn Valley in which Widecombe sits. North-east is Haytor, with Rippon Tor slightly south of due east. To the south the view is dominated by Pil Tor, the next objective.

The Ruggle Stone, near Widecombe-in-the-Moor

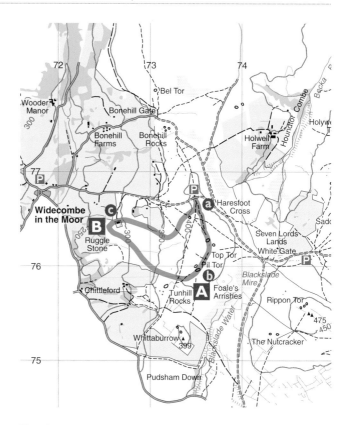

Now head south-south-west, taking the broad, gently falling ridge to Pil Tor. South from here the ground falls away to Buckland Common at the edge of which stands the picturesque village of Buckland-in-the-Moor. To the east of Pil Tor lies Foale's Arrishes (737758).

A Foale's Arrishes
In summer the ancient settlement of Foale's Arrishes can be difficult to pick out among the bracken, but those who persevere will find the remains of about eight huts and divided enclosure walls. Excavations suggest several places of occupation, the last being very late Bronze Age, the period just before the arrival of iron-using folk. The curious name of the settlement derives from Foale, a one-time owner of the local land and the old dialect name for a cereal field.

b From the settlement return to Pil Tor and head west. To the left are Tunhill Rocks below the eastern edge of which are the remains of another small Bronze Age settlement. Here, in addition to the normal circular huts there is one that is rectangular, a very unusual feature as it is more difficult to roof such a building.

At the wall elbow, bear half right and descend north-west across the moor. There is a walled enclosure on the right; continue north-westwards into an area of moor with field walls on both sides, soon reaching the Ruggle Stone (726765).

B Ruggle Stone

The Ruggle Stone is a logan or logging rock. Natural erosion occasionally causes a large boulder to be perched on another, or on bedrock, by a single point of contact directly under the centre of gravity of the boulder. In that case the slightest touch will cause the perched boulder to rock gently. Logans were claimed to tell the future to anyone with the ability to interpret the rock's motion after they had asked it a question and set it in motion. Local legend maintains that the Ruggle Stone can only be set in motion by someone holding a church door key.

There are several logans on Dartmoor, one of which – on the south-western side of nearby Rippon Tor a short distance south-east of the present route – is named Nut Crackers on OS maps. Legend has it that the locals used the rocking stone to crack nuts, though the distance of the stone from any villages or farms suggests that the name is more likely to derive from the locals having a laugh at the expense of a visitor.

c From the Ruggle Stone head east-south-east, climbing to Hollow Tor (731762). Now turn north-east, climbing across open moor and passing the Shovel Stone (733763), another large boulder. Maintain direction to return to the start.

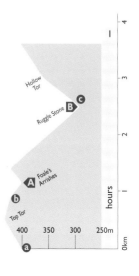

Please note: time taken calculated according to the Naismith Formula (see p.2)

LUSTLEIGH CLEAVE

MAPS:
OS Landranger Sheet 191, OS Outdoor Leisure Sheet 28

START/FINISH:
Lustleigh church 785813. There is no car park in the village and in summer it can be overflowing with cars, particularly at weekends. Spring and autumn in the cleave are marvellous alternatives: in summer try to arrive early and please park considerately

DevonBus 173 (Newton Abbot to Okehampton via Moretonhampstead) stops at Lustleigh

DISTANCE/ASCENT:
8 miles (11km)/1,600ft (480m)

APPROXIMATE TIME:
3 hours

HIGHEST POINT:
Hunter's Tor 1,069ft (326m)

REFRESHMENTS:
There are two options in Lustleigh: the Cleave Inn and the Primrose Café

ADVICE:
A straightforward walk, but with a sharp ascent to Hunter's Tor. The riverside path can be muddy after wet weather

To the north-east of Hound Tor the River Bovey flows through a tight, thickly-wooded gorge – a cleave in the local dialect. This walk starts at the picture postcard pretty village of Lustleigh, then follows the river's path through the cleave, returning to the village across a fine section of moorland.

A Lustleigh

There has been a settlement here since Saxon times, a record from the time of Edward the Confessor notes that the manor was held by a man called Esgart. The Domesday Book notes the manor's transfer to Ansgar, the Conqueror's head cook, and that Lustleigh was the only village in Devon to have a bee-keeper.

The village church is a neat building with a sturdy square tower. Its earliest part, the porch, dates from the 13th century, much of the rest dating from a 15th century rebuild. Inside there are several fine effigies, including those of Sir Robert Dynham and his wife. Sir Robert was Lord of the Manor in the late 13th century. The effigy of Sir William le Prous is a little later, Sir William dying in 1316. The most interesting item is an engraved gravestone. The inscription is Celtic, though as the Celts had no written language it is likely to be post-Roman, and has been translated as reading 'The memorial of Datuidoc the son of Cohinoc'.

Lustleigh's May Day, held on the first Saturday in May, is one of the most colourful in Devon. The May Queen leads a procession of maypole dancers around the village beneath a canopy of flowers held aloft by four canopy bearers before being crowned with a crown of flowers on a granite boulder in the Town Orchard (across from the church) on which her name is then inscribed. Close to the church is the old Church House (see Note to Walk 17) dating from the 14th century.

a From the church cross the road and head east along the famous Wreyland Path, under the old railway bridge until you meet a minor road which you follow for a few metres, passing a road on the left, and then taking a right turn where the road continues straight ahead. Follow the side road until you reach a field path heading to the south-west. Follow this down into a wooded valley, passing by a small sewage works, and then heading uphill, under the old railway track, to a road (786808).

Turn left and then right into a short length of track (785808) which leads to another lane. Turn left into this lane and in a few metres turn right into a steep, surfaced bridleway. Follow the bridleway to Hisley Farm, using gates into and out of the farm buildings and continuing along a path that descends through woodland, bearing round to the right to reach Hisley Bridge, a single-arched packhorse bridge buried deep in the Bovey valley.

Cross the bridge to a wide track and turn right, getting further west of the river, until you reach a path on the right (776802). Take this path over the bridge crossing the Becka Brook. The path then heads north-west through Houndtor Wood, following the west bank of the Bovey to Clambridge (767811).

B Houndtor Wood

Viewed from Trendlebere Down (beside the road that links Bovey Tracey with Manaton) the valley of the River Bovey – to the north of the Down – is a sea of trees. This is Houndtor Wood, one of Dartmoor's finest sections of mixed deciduous woodland. Virtually all British broadleaf trees are represented here, making it ideal for insects and birds. Great, blue, marsh and long-tailed tits may be seen, together with chiffchaffs, blackcaps and tree pipits. The wood also has pairs of nesting woodcocks. Of the rarer residents, the lucky walker may see

Lustleigh village on eastern Dartmoor

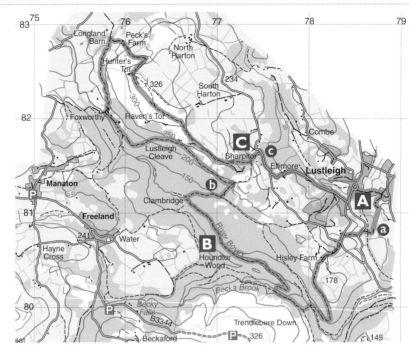

the lesser spotted woodpecker. Dippers can usually be seen working the stream, with grey wagtails at the water's edge.

b Cross Clambridge and follow the main path opposite climbing north-east towards Sharpitor and passing two paths on the right. At the next intersection (772813), below the woods under Sharpitor, take the path left, passing the old mill (759818), then on to the thatched cottages of Foxworthy (758821). Here, bear half right to follow a signed, and

Houndtor Wood and Lustleigh Cleave from Trendlebere Down

sometimes wet, bridleway towards Peck Farm. At a track junction (758828) with Longland Barn, ahead, turn right to reach Peck Farm. Go through a gate beyond the farm and cross a field to another gate. Maintain direction to reach a gate in a crossing wall. Do not go through: instead, turn right, walking with the wall on your left at first, to reach Hunter's Tor (761825), an excellent viewpoint. The tor is topped by an Iron Age hillfort.

From the tor, stay to the right-hand side of the broad ridge descending south-eastwards, with continuing fine views into the wooded cleave to the right. Be cautious on this section of the walk: it is said locally that this ridge is haunted by a ghostly Roman legion. There is little evidence for a sigificant Roman presence in Lustleigh bar the discovery of a few coins, nevertheless the story persists.

There is a path on the ridge, faint enough to imply that ghostly feet pass very gently, but the way is obvious, if occasionally made difficult by the gorse. Go past Raven's Tor and Harton Chest, another tor, both on the right, to reach Sharpitor (772815).

C Sharpitor

At Sharpitor the OS notes the existence of Nut Crackers (Logan Stone). Most guides point out that this is out of date, the stone in question having been vandalised. It was, it is said, a superb logan (see Note to Walk 14) whose rocking could be used to crack nuts. Then drunken vandals trundled the logan down into the cleave, breaking off a section. The outraged locals attempted to haul it back up to Sharpitor, but the attempt failed when the stone broke again and any further attempt was abandoned, leaving only the name for posterity. However, the villagers claim that this story is untrue and that the logan rocks still – though now it is difficult to find amongst the undergrowth. It was, apparently, the more prominent Christening Stone which was vandalised. The stone was so-called because it had a rock basin (see Note to Walk 6) which had been used to hold holy water for open-air Christenings.

c   The path descends east-north-east past Sharpitor reaching a path junction (774816) where you turn left (NE) along the path to the road at Hammerslake (775816), turning right along the road. Follow the road until you reach the first junction, and turn left, descending steeply to pass Ellimore, then sharply again to reach the Lustleigh Baptist Church at a T-junction. Turn left and return to the start.

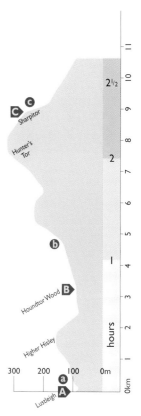

Please note: time taken calculated according to the Naismith Formula (see p.2)

HOUND TOR AND BECKY FALLS

MAPS:
OS Landranger Sheet 191, OS Outdoor Leisure Sheet 28

START/FINISH:
There are several possibilities, with car parks at Becky Falls (at 758800) and Swallerton Gate (at 739792). A short detour also allows the car park at Manaton (at 750812) to be used. The walk description below assumes a start at Swallerton Gate

DevonBus 671, which links Whiddon Down to Newton Abbot via Moretonhampstead, stops at Manaton. The bus runs only on Wednesday and Friday (but not Good Friday)

DISTANCE/ASCENT:
8 miles (13km)/1,300ft (400m)

APPROXIMATE TIME:
4 hours

HIGHEST POINT:
Hound Tor 1,358ft (414m)

REFRESHMENTS:
There is an inn at Manaton and a cafe at Becky Falls, but best is the refreshment van at the Swallerton Gate car park. How is it possible to resist a tea or coffee from the 'Hound of the Basket Meals'? (Open throughout spring and summer but at weekends autumn and winter, weather permitting)

N ear Manaton, a village sitting above the River Bovey on the western side of the moor, are two sites with compelling stories, one mythical, though appealing, the other enigmatic and based on truth. This route threads a route around them and visits a famous tor and a beautiful waterfall.

a   From the car park cross the road and follow the broad swathe of grass uphill south-east to Hound Tor. The summit has three distinct tors, a small one – known by climbers as Perched Block – to the right as you climb – then two large ones separated by a grassy strip. The one on the left is the Hound's Head, though a good imagination is needed to see a dog's outline among the blocks. Follow the avenue to its southern end from where the first half of the route can be seen. In the distance is Haytor. Closer are Greator Rocks with the low walls of the medieval village nestling below it. Not easily visible from here, but lying slightly west of the southern tor is a cairn circle, a small stone circle around a kistvaen, a rock-slab box for cremated remains. The site dates from the Bronze Age.

From the end of the grass avenue between the tors of Hound Tor, go down any of the broad grassy strips to the medieval village (746788). In spring and early summer your walk will be accompanied by the haunting call of meadow pipits 'parachuting' to earth.

Hound Tor

The route to the medieval village from Hound Tor

A   Medieval Village

It is believed that there was a settlement on the well-sheltered, fertile land between Hound Tor and Greator Rocks as early as the 8th century, and there was certainly one at the time of the Domesday Book which noted that it belonged to the Abbot of Tavistock. What remains dates from the 13th or early 14th centuries and comprises eleven buildings – at least three inhabited longhouses and a collection of outbuildings. The outbuildings were probably a mix of dairy, cow sheds and storage barns. In three of them kilns have been discovered, implying the drying of corn for long term storage. The longhouses were for both village folk and their animals. They were stone-walled with a roof of thatch or turf supported by wooden poles. The animals and people shared a common entrance to the house, the stock occupying one end, the people the other. The living area was raised above the byre and separated by a wooden fence. The living area had a further raised area for sleeping, the lower section being used for cooking with smoke from the fire disappearing through a conveniently placed hole in the roof. With smoke from back draughts, the lack of light as there were no windows, the cold, draughts from the door and inadequate roof sealing, and the noise and smell of the cattle, it is unlikely that early medieval living quite matched the occasionally portrayed idyll of folk close to, and in tune with, their environment.

It is not clear why the village was deserted, but the last phase of occupation coincides with the arrival of the Black Death in 1346 so it seems likely that the villagers died out. The village

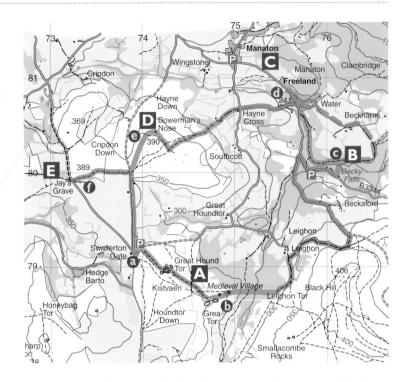

was also an upland settlement and changes in climate or agricultural methods may have persuaded the inhabitants to move to a lower site. Perhaps it was a combination of the two, the plague killing some villagers and forcing others to leave, the difficulties of farming the area persuading them that returning to their village was not worthwhile.

Hound Tor village's folk were subsistence farmers constantly living on the edge of disaster from crop failure and prone to early deaths from accident or illness. It would be interesting to know if they took as much pleasure in the beauty of their surroundings as the walkers who now wander through their longhouses.

b　From the village continue east along the clear path, bearing left and going through several wall gaps and a signed gate, with the picturesque rowan- and hawthorn-clad mass of Greator Rocks off to the right. The well-marked path descends steeply, then crosses a clapper bridge (752788) over Becka Brook, and climbs above the woods, with Smallacombe Rocks off to the right and Black Hill ahead. Turn left (NE) on a good contouring path, and down a gated track to Leighon (756792) an estate to the left. Here you take the right fork, for Upper Terrace Drive, contouring east-north-east around Black Hill with a series of 'newtakes' – fields of reclaimed moorland – on the left. Follow the track to reach an unfenced minor road. Turn left and follow the road over the cattle grid, going north-west steeply downhill and over Beckaford Bridge to reach a T-junction with the B3387. Turn right for a short walk along the road – please take care, the road can be very busy in summer and at weekends.

Those wanting entrance tickets for the falls need to continue down the road, across New Bridge, and past the car park (right) to the shop and cafe, from where they will proceed to the elevated walkway and turn right for the falls. The network of trails through the private estate offers further exploration to those who wish it, but complicates identification of the public path because of the overlapping and contiguous trails.

If not wishing to visit the falls as a ticket holder, follow the road only as far as the public path to the left (757801) just before New Bridge. Take this path, crossing over the stream by the footbridge, and a few metres on, turn right on to a cross path which runs above the Becka Brook. The path travels west and south-west and emerges alongside an elevated walkway from the cafe and shop and continues east past the private way down to the falls.

B   Becky Falls

The first thing to decide is what is the real name for the falls – is it 'Becka' or 'Becky'? The answer seems to be both. At some point, many years ago, it is assumed that the northern word beck for a fast flowing stream was applied to the one draining down from Hound Tor to the River Bovey in Lustleigh Cleave. Over time the locals expanded the name to Becka and Becky. Becka is preferred by the OS, and is seen in Beckaford Bridge, but Becky has a long pedigree, having been used by Victorian visitors to the falls and is preferred by the current owners of the estate on which it is found. There are local stories about a girl called Becky, but these are contrived and contradictory, and clearly recent inventions.

The falls are a boulder 'tumble' rather than a conventional falls (such as White Lady in Lydford Gorge – see Walk 1) created by the undercutting of a band of metamorphic rock. Metamorphic rock is created when molten magma flows close to sedimentary rock, in this case as the granites of Dartmoor were forced to the surface. Stream water seeping into the

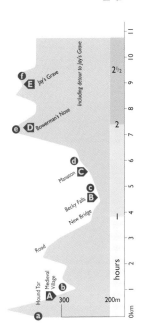

Please note: time taken calculated according to the Naismith Formula (see p.2)

Becky Falls

cracks in the metamorphic rock causes frost shattering with boulders being broken off and deposited on the stream bed. The water-smoothed boulders create the ruckle down which Beckabrook tumbles. Though less spectacular than a conventional falls, Becky is a marvellous sight, especially when rain has swollen Beckabrook. In summer, when the water flow is less, the moss-encrusted boulders, lit by sunlight flashing through the surrounding trees, is equally attractive.

There is a superb piece of woodland around the falls, a part of Houndtor Wood – which stretches all the way into the Bovey valley – which is being carefully managed to create diverse habitats for birds and plants. The wood is chiefly oak, with beech, ash and sycamore, and areas of alder, birch and willow. Within the woods there are beds of bluebells, with scatterings of wood sorrel and primroses, but also more unusual species – yellow pimpernel, bugle, cuckoo flower (lady's smock), opposite-leaved golden saxifrage and slender St John's wort. The wood attracts a small number of butterfly species: most summer visitors will see the speckled wood, the luckier walker also seeing silver washed fritillary or purple hairstreak.

The woodland birds include treecreepers, nuthatches, pied and spotted flycatchers, goldcrests and woodcock. Dippers can be seen in Beckabrook. An attempt is being made to re-establish the otter.

c Whichever way you have come, you have, after viewing, the option of continuing eastward on the public path through Deal Copse until it intersects the way up from Hisley Bridge (at 766803) and of taking the turning to the left to Beckhams, where a quiet road takes you west-south-west to the Kestor Inn (757807). Alternatively, you can retrace your steps along the public path, at first westwards but veering north through the woods. The way passes the path, to the left, by which you originally approached from the road (758802). Continue northwards, ignoring a turning on the right, as far as the road just south of Water. Turn right along the road to the Kestor Inn.

C Manaton

Technically the Kestor Inn is in Freeland, the 'true' village of Manaton lying another ½ mile (800m) along the road. It is a pretty village, worth a visit if you have the time for a detour. The church is 15th century but needed considerable restoration after being battered by a storm of legendary strength in 1779. Outside the church stands the stump of an old cross. The locals carried coffins three times around the cross to disorientate the spirit of the dead – and so prevent it pestering the living – a tradition which so upset a late 19th century vicar he removed the stump, using it as the base of a stile. Only after many years was the cross rediscovered and re-erected, though the theft does seem to have put an end to the tradition. The church has a fine 16th century rood screen: this, too, has needed restoration, though here the damage was by human (Puritan) hand during the Civil War. To the south-west of Manaton is Wingstone Farm where John Galsworthy lived for 18 years. It was at the farm that he wrote *The Forsyte Saga*.

d Opposite the inn is a turning, beside the Post Office, signed for Southcott: take this, following it westwards to the cross-roads at Hayne Cross. Go straight over, following a metalled lane that soon becomes a stony track. Continue to a

Bowerman's Nose, the distinctive tor on Hayne Down

The flowers on Jay's Grave are said to be laid by a ghostly hand

gate on to open moorland and maintain direction along a bridleway that climbs to the high point of Hayne Down. From here head north-west to reach the prominent tor of Bowerman's Nose.

D   Bowerman's Nose

The Nose is a tor which, in profile, looks like a man wearing a peaked cap. The name is the subject of debate and of one of the moor's most delightful legends. It is likely that there really was a John Bowerman who lived in the 17th century and was buried in North Bovey churchyard. Could he have had a distinctive, angular profile which led folk to name the tor for him? The legend may date from Bowerman's time, though many claim it pre-dates him. It concerns another man called Bowerman, a fine hunter from Manaton who frequently hunted hares and birds on Hayne Down. One day while hunting he stealthily moved through the shrub cover on the moor and was surprised to see a coven of witches dancing on the moor. Given that this occurred in medieval times it might be expected that Bowerman rushed back to the village and prepared for a burning at the stake. In fact he jumped up and shouted, scattering the terrified witches whose black arts clearly did not extend to foretelling the immediate future or coping with surprises. Bowerman left the moor chuckling over his trick.

Some days later Bowerman was out hunting again and caught sight of a magnificent hare which he stalked on to the high part of the moor, overlooking the village. As he drew closer to the hare and prepared his bow and arrow, the hare turned into one of the witches he had surprised. She raised a bony finger in his direction, muttered a spell and disappeared. When

Bowerman tried to move he found he had been encased in granite. He could see out towards the village but could neither move nor shout. When his friends and family came to the moor to look for him he could see them frantically searching the moor but could do nothing to attract their attention. Fully conscious Bowerman watched in despair as their searches became less frequent and then stopped altogether. Poor Bowerman is still entombed in the tor, still watching as folk enjoy themselves around him, the witch's curse condemning him to an eternity of frustration.

e From the high point of Hayne Down head south-west, with Hound Tor off to the left, to reach an unfenced minor road (739800). Turn left along this. The road leads back to Swallerton Gate and the car park, but a detour is worthwhile, taking the track on the right at Moyle's Gate (opposite the farm). Follow the track west over Swine Down to reach another road and Jay's Grave (732799).

D Jay's Grave

Kitty Jay was the daughter of a tenant farmer who fell in love with the landowner's son and, persuaded by his stories of love, marriage and a life of happiness, was seduced by him. When, after a long night of passion, she reminded him of his promises he laughed at her, telling her he would never marry so lowly a person, nor one who could contemplate sex before marriage. Kitty went home and after a long day of inconsolable sadness hanged herself in her father's barn. Suicides were not allowed a Christian burial and their spirits were feared by local folk. Kitty was therefore buried without ceremony at this crossroads, the hope being that her spirit, confused by the number of roads, would not wander and so would be unable to plague the neighbourhood. The cross-road burial therefore performed the same function as the procession of coffins around the Manaton cross.

Many years later a man wanting to know the truth of the story excavated the grave site and found that it did indeed contain the skeleton of a young woman. The man created the grave we now see, with its simple headstone. There the story would have ended, but it is said that flowers are regularly placed on the grave by a ghostly hand and that those who stay at the crossroads at night to try to watch are driven away by perceived terrors before the flowers arrive.

f From Jay's Grave, reverse the route to Moyle's Gate and turn right to return along the road to the start.

WIDECOMBE AND HAMEL DOWN

MAPS:
Harvey Dartmoor North, OS Landranger Sheet 191, OS Outdoor Leisure Sheet 28

START/FINISH:
At 719769, the car park at the eastern end of Widecombe-in-the-Moor. There is a seasonal (fee) car park further along the road into the village, beside the road to Natsworthy

DevonBuses 170 and 171, which take circular routes from Newton Abbot, stop at Widecombe. The buses run only on Sundays and Public Holidays. DevonBus 672, which links Buckland in the Moor with Newton Abbot, stops at Widecombe and runs only on Wednesday

DISTANCE/ASCENT:
8¾ miles (14km)/1,560ft (485m)

APPROXIMATE TIME:
3½ hours

HIGHEST POINT:
Broad Barrow, Hamel Down 1,745ft (532m)

REFRESHMENTS:
There are numerous possibilities in Widecombe

ADVICE:
Easy walking, but with a long climb from the village to start. Care needed on the final descent, by road, into the village

Widecombe-in-the-Moor is the most famous of all Dartmoor villages and will be on the itinerary of all visitors to the moor. Set in a fertile valley and, consequently, surrounded by fields, it is not, however, the easiest place to use as a centre for walking. Here, using short sections of minor road a fine walk is organised incorporating Hamel Down, to the north-west of the village.

A Widecombe-in-the-Moor

There is more to the village than old Tom Cobley and all, though you could be forgiven for not thinking so as you gaze at the plethora of potential souvenirs. The church is late 14th century and has one of the finest towers in Devon, paid for by local tin miners and a tribute to the wealth generated by Dartmoor's metal ore. The tower is 135ft (41m) high and its grandeur has caused Widecombe church to be referred to as Dartmoor's cathedral. In 1638 during the service on Sunday 21 October, at the height of one of the most ferocious storms known on the moor, a 'bolt of fire' (lightning, or an example of the still little understood ball lightning?) hit the tower, knocking off one of the pinnacles. The falling pinnacle went through the roof of the church. Four of the congregation were killed, though a contemporary record claims they were killed not by the pinnacle, but by a fiery ball that passed through the church at the same time. Was this the same lightning ball?

A local legend claims that the toppling of the tower was not due to the storm or lightning, but the result of a deadly game played by Jan Reynolds, a local man. Jan is said to have borrowed money from the Devil in order to pay gambling debts. On that fateful Sunday the Devil was due to meet Jan in the inn at Poundsgate, to the south of Widecombe. However, when the Devil arrived he found that Jan had gone to church at Widecombe. The Devil rode his black horse to Widecombe, marched into the church and hauled Jan out. As he was carried up into the air a trailing foot (or cloven hoof) detached the pinnacle. Jan was carrying his playing cards in his pocket and the ride through the sky caused four – the four aces – to fall to the ground. On the southern flank of Birch Tor, to the north-west of Hameldown Tor, there are four fields still known as the Four Aces.

Beside the church is Church House. Church Houses, often called church ale-houses, were built as church halls and village meeting rooms. They would also be used as brew houses, the beer being sold, together with food, to the congregation. This was particularly welcomed by folk who had travelled from outlying farms. The profits from the sales helped towards the upkeep of the church. Widecombe's house, which dates to 1537, is one of few that remain and is now in the care of the National Trust, though it remains the village hall. Next door is the old Sexton's Cottage which is now an Information Centre for the National Park.

The song which has made Widecombe famous refers to Dartmoor's most famous fair, a medieval livestock market to which folk came from all over the moor. The men mentioned in the song – Bill Brewer, Jan Stewer, Peter Gurney, Peter Davy, Daniel Whiddon, Harry Hawke, Tom Cobley of course, and not forgetting Tom Pearce whose 'old grey mare' was needed by the

Widecombe-in-the-Moor nestled below jagged tors

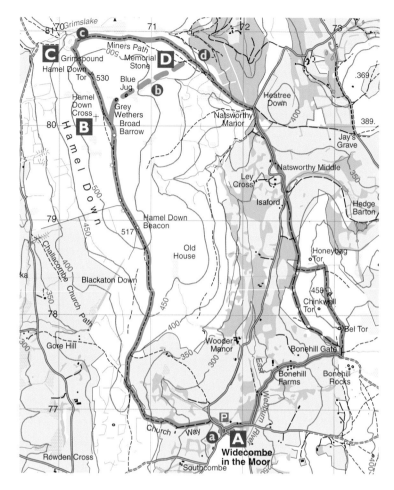

singer – were from outside Widecombe and travelling to it to do business. The song is traditional, but was only written down in the late 19th century (by the famous Dartmoor cleric, Rev Sabine Baring-Gould, vicar of Lew Trenchard). It soon became popular and helped to promote Widecombe as a tourist centre. Today the fair still flourishes: it is held on the second Tuesday of September, but is now more gymkhana, livestock show and funfair than a real market.

a Widecombe really is set high on the moor – a local saying for when it is snowing is that Widecombe folk are plucking their geese – but despite that our walk starts with a long climb. After parking your car, return to the car park entrance and take the path to the right. This leads to the Natsworthy road, as confirmed by the signpost. Follow it for about 200 yards (183m) to reach Church Lane, on the left. Take this, climbing steadily westwards to its end – the road becomes a track – where a fine pair of stone gateposts mark the start of open moorland. Continue climbing, now to the north, following the wall on the right, to reach the broad ridge that is the southern extremity of Hamel Down. The wall on the right turns eastwards. Continue on the path in a northerly direction, observing any diversions for erosion control purposes, which the National Park Authority is forced to impose from time to time. You are now on a section of the Two Moors Way (see Note to Walk 25).

Follow the path uphill to the summit of Hameldown Beacon, (708789), an excellent viewpoint of the high central moorland to the west and of the distinctive tors to the east. From the Beacon, continue along the gently rising ridge, passing a series of Bronze Age burial chambers, their names (you may notice that the spelling on the stones differs from that on modern-day OS maps) being marked on adjacent stones. Go past Two Barrows, Single Barrow and at Broad Barrow (706799) – unless doing the shorter version of the walk, see para b below – take the left of the two tracks to pass Hamel Down Cross (704801) on your left. Continue on this path to reach Hameldown Tor (703806) and Grimspound.

B   Hamel Down Cross

The cross, or what remains of it, is at least medieval, perhaps older, and marked an ancient route across the eastern edge of the moor – a forerunner of the Two Moors Way. Such crosses were not only waymarkers but marked the top of significant climbs. As a result they were often known as 'Thank God' crosses, the traveller struggling uphill and then uttering thanks as he paused to rest at the cross. The cross is inscribed HC DS 1854, a piece of vandalism to which 150 years have lent an air of respectability. The inscription means 'Hamel Cross, Duke of Somerset'. The Duke owned Natsworthy Manor (passed later in the walk) and wanted to indicate the boundaries of the manorial estate. The Duke was also responsible for the erection of the name stones on the barrows on Hamel Down, these also representing the boundaries of his estate. There are two further boundary stones to the north-east of the cross, known as Grey Wether (because the stone looks like a grazing sheep – see Note to Walk 7) and Blue Jug. The latter marks the source of the East Webburn River which flows past Natsworthy Manor and in whose valley Widecombe stands.

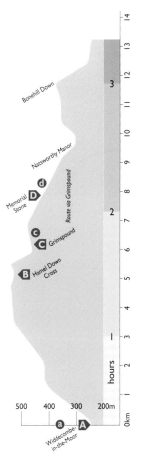

Please note: time taken calculated according to the Naismith Formula (see p.2)

The curious wooden posts on Hamel Down are not related to the Duke of Somerset's estate but were erected in 1940 when it was feared the Down could be used by a German invasion force landing in gliders. Many of the posts have rotted or fallen as a result of being used as rubbing posts by sheep, but some remain to baffle the walker.

b   For the shorter route, fork right (N) from Broad Barrow as far as a nearby dip in the land (705802); here turn right onto a tiny path (at 240° from Hamel Down Cross), soon descending north-east and traversing a wet area, passing the Grey Wethers (706803) and Blue Jug (707803) boundary stones (on your right). The path continues down the steepening valley, left of the stream (East Webburn River), but bear left (NE) near the lower end of the small ravine (711805) to an intersecting track and the RAF Memorial (712806). Turn right to join the track from Grimspound to Natsworthy Corner.

C   Grimspound

Grimspound is the best preserved Bronze Age settlement on Dartmoor, its relative remoteness and large site meaning it has survived the plundering such sites suffered – they were very convenient quarries for locals building farmhouses or walls – better than most. Its retaining wall is almost 9ft (over 2.5m) thick and is thought to have been at least 6ft (nearly 2m) high when completed. The wall encloses an area of about 4 acres. Inside are the remains of 24 huts, each of familiar Bronze Age form – a circular wall about 15ft (5m) in diameter from which a conical thatch or turf roof would have risen to a centrally mounted pole. Note the small cross inscribed on the right hand pillar at the entrance to the pound, which is paved with slabs, presumably to avoid the accumulation of deep mud. This implies significant traffic, presumably livestock which were taken out on to the moor each day to forage and brought back each night. The enclosing wall was therefore designed as protection, but a protection against what? The pound is hardly in a good position if protection was required against marauding bands of men, so it is assumed that it was to prevent the livestock from falling prey to the wolves and bears which inhabited Bronze Age Dartmoor.

From Bonehill Rocks looking towards Hameldown

The pound's name is thought to be Saxon, Grim being synonymous with the Norse god Odin. However, as Grim was also a local name for the Devil, it is possible that locals, not understanding the origins of the site, named it for a supernatural builder.

c From Grimspound follow the track, climbing slightly and heading east on to the broad plateau that links Hameldown Tor and King Tor (the mound on top being King's Barrow), to the left. The path then descends a broad spur of moor, with the East Webburn River off to the right. As a wall elbow is approached a track leads off to the right. Along this track is a memorial stone.

D Memorial Stone

The stone is inscribed RAF S49 RDW CJL RB RLAE 21.3.41. It was at this spot on 21 March 1941 that a Handley Page Hampden bomber of RAF 49 Squadron crashed with the loss of its four crew, RD Wilson, CJ Lyon, R Brenes and RLA Ellis. The stone was erected by the mother of RD Wilson, the pilot.

d From the Memorial, return to the main track and continue south-east to reach a minor road at Natsworthy Gate. Turn right (SSE), soon passing Natsworthy Manor to the right. Follow the road to where it bends right – with a track turning off to the left – and there maintain direction, taking a field path short cut to regain the road. Continue along the road, going downhill past West Lodge. At a cattle grid an old quarry track goes off left (724788); take this, climbing steeply towards Honeybag Tor and passing through a gate. At a point midway under the two tors above (726785), where you can, if you have already had enough climbing, continue along the mine track to Bonehill, take the prominent grass path climbing steeply east. Turn left at the col so as to appreciate the views from Honeybag Tor. Return south to the col and continue on good paths along the ridge, passing Chinkwell and Bell Tors, then descend to the road by Bonehill Rocks (731775). This takes you steeply down westwards, through the hamlet of Bonehill, to Widecombe-in-the-Moor and the start.

BUCKFAST ABBEY

MAPS:
OS Landranger Sheets 202, OS Outdoor Leisure Sheet 28

START/FINISH:
There are car parks at Buckfast Abbey (741673) and at the Mill Abbey Inn in Buckfast, each of which can be used with permission. Parking is also available in Buckfastleigh, but please park considerately

Several buses serve Buckfastleigh and Buckfast Abbey. Stagecoach buses 39 and X39 stop at Buckfastleigh, while Western National bus X88 stops at both the village and the abbey. DevonBus 165 also stops at both. DevonBuses 170 and 171 stop at both, but run only on Sundays and Public Holidays

DISTANCE/ASCENT:
4½ miles (7.5km)/394ft (120m)

APPROXIMATE TIME:
2 hours

HIGHEST POINT:
Button Farm 450ft (137m)

REFRESHMENTS:
There is a café/restaurant at Buckfast Abbey and inns at both Buckfast and Buckfastleigh

ADVICE:
Much of the walk is on minor roads or through villages. These are sometimes busy and occasionally narrow so please take care

At the south-eastern edge of the National Park, close to the River Dart, stands Buckfast Abbey, one of Dartmoor's most popular visitor sites. This walk takes in the abbey and the nearby village of Buckfast and Buckfastleigh.

A Buckfast Abbey

Although the famed abbey at Glastonbury was responsible for the founding of several abbeys on the South-West Peninsula during the 10th century there is no firm evidence for the founding of Buckfast before 1018 when Aethelweard, an Earl under King Cnut, founded (or refounded) the abbey for Benedictine monks. Buckfast does not seem to have been very successful, the number of monks falling and the abbey losing some of its land holdings within a few years of this founding. The decline continued after the Norman Conquest, but was reversed in spectacular style in 1147 when the abbey became a Cistercian house. The Cistercian order had begun at Cîteaux in Burgundy, its monks returning to the strict rules of St Benedict which they saw as having lapsed over the centuries since the saint's death. The Cistercian lifestyle was ferocious in its workload, the monks having little time for leisure or idleness in a punishing schedule of work and prayer. But the result of their industry was the creation of the English wool industry as the monks developed sheep farming on their holdings.

The Buckfast monks encouraged sheep rearing on their Dartmoor estates and cereal farming on their more fertile lands. Dartmoor fleeces were not of the best quality, sheep (then as now) having a harder time on the moor than they did, say, on the Cotswolds, the heart of the English wool trade, but cereal production obviously fared better, requiring the building of the large grange barn near the medieval north gate.

The Cistercians rebuilt the Saxon abbey in stone, Buckfast following the order's conventional design with the abbey church, cloisters and monks' building grouped together, and a collection of outbuildings – guest quarters, stables, gatehouses, barns etc. – set close by. Under the Cistercians Buckfast flourished, the income from its land holdings being

Buckfast Abbey from the abbey's Physic Garden

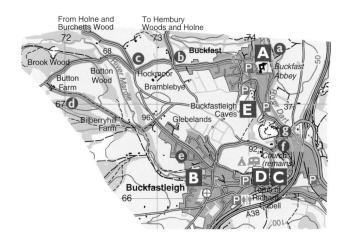

enhanced by a series of bequests from local lords. Now, almost a thousand years from the greatest flourishing of monasticism in England, it is difficult to fully comprehend the place of the monasteries in society, but it seems that the lords were able to 'buy' their way to Heaven for a relatively small outlay (or, perhaps, to buy the quiescence of their peasants) while continuing with what was, in the main, distinctly un-Christian behaviour; and that the peasants had both their spiritual needs and their religious observances carried out by proxy, leaving them to toil day-long, as their tenancies required. The system worked well, but as the wealth of the abbeys increased so did their power. And as the power of individual abbots increased, so did their willingness to exercise it (and to slip into a life of luxury). At the height of English monasticism (in the 13th century) it is estimated that there was one monk to every 150 head of population. By the 16th century the ratio had fallen to 1 in 250, yet the wealth of the monasteries had increased dramatically: they now controlled more than 25 per cent of the land.

Such was their power and wealth that they frightened kings, and Henry VIII, having broken with the Pope over his divorce from Catherine of Aragon, readily agreed to his new Protestant church hierarchy suppressing the monasteries, confiscating their wealth and eliminating their power. The Dissolution of the Monasteries began in 1536 and ended in 1540; Buckfast was dissolved on 25 February 1539.

As was usual, the abbey's roof lead was melted down and sold, the stonework used as a convenient quarry. The buildings, partially demolished and roofless, were then assaulted by the elements, though such had been the quality of the building that 250 years later the ruins, as depicted in contemporary drawings, were still impressive. Then, in 1806, much of what remained was demolished to make way for a mansion built by Samuel Berry, a local mill owner. The mansion's construction bankrupted Berry and, in 1882, a subsequent owner offered it to the Catholic church. Soon the building had been taken over by a group of French Benedictine monks. The first abbot of the new abbey was drowned when the ship he was travelling in was wrecked off the Spanish coast. It was therefore left to his successor to build the abbey's new church. This was accomplished over a 30-year period to 1937 (though the church was consecrated in 1932) by a team of just four monks using manual rope hoists to raise the stone, a truly remarkable feat. Today the church can be visited daily; outside it is a dignified building, its design echoing medieval themes; inside it has elegant, soaring lines. Close by are two formal gardens, one of herbs, the other a 'pleasure' garden where the church can be viewed to an accompaniment of the murmuring River Dart. The abbey has a restaurant and a book shop, and a gift shop which sells, among other things, the famous Buckfast honey and tonic wine.

a   From the Abbey car park (741673), return to the road and turn left, first northwards and then sharply left (W) along Grange Road to Fritz's grave, by a T-junction. Turn right towards Hembury Woods, and shortly you will come to a road to the left (732674). From here, there are two options: the first, just a short walk in the outskirts of Buckfast; the second, adding 4½ miles (7.25km), a longer country walk taking in the attractive village of Holne. Both walks link up again at Hockmoor crossroads (727673). Please note this longer walk does not appear in full on the map shown here.

b   For the village of Holne, continue from Fritz's Grave northwards along the Holne Road to a byway near the bottom of Hembury Woods N.T. (at 729681). Turn left along the byway heading west-north-west through N.T. woodlands, then alongside Holy Brook, turning north-north-west to Shuttaford (719692). Turn left into a lane heading west-north-west for the village of Holne. Continue west-north-west past Ridgey cross. From Holne turn left (S) before the church and pub, and go to a road junction (706693). Take the left turn south (for Scorriton) and soon, where the road bears right, keep straight on down a byway on the left, reaching a lane at Langaford (708687). Turn left along the lane, and shortly take a field path on the right (709687), east-south-east to Mill Leat

Please note: time taken calculated according to the Naismith Formula (see p.2)

Squire Cabell's tomb in the churchyard of Holy Trinity Church

(713685). Go down the lane to the right but, in a few yards, just after crossing the bridge over Holy Brook, turn left into a bridleway, east, continuing through Burchett's Wood to the Holne Road. Then bear left (ESE) to the crossroads at Hockmoor (727673).

c   From the Hockmoor crossroads, turn sharply right (from Holne), or half right (from Buckfast) to go north-west along the road towards Bowerdon and Bowden, signposted Hockmoor Hand, crossing the Mardle, climbing steeply between Button Wood and Brook Wood up to Button Farm (718673).

d   Now follow the track ahead to a lane, but, soon after, another lane joins from the right; go left through a kissing gate and cross a field to a footbridge over the River Mardle (728667). Beyond the bridge follow a path over a stile and into woodland, bearing right, uphill. At the first junction turn sharp left and then take the right-hand branch at the Y-junction ahead of you. The path leads upwards to a lane which opens onto the road opposite the Buckfastleigh Cricket and Rugby Ground. Turn right and follow the road into Buckfastleigh.

B   Buckfastleigh

Buckfastleigh is a delightful Devonian town, virtually untouched by tourism despite Buckfast Abbey being one of the county's most visited sites and the other nearby attractions. The town grew prosperous on woollen mills and leather tanning, the mills powered by the River Mardle, the tanning industry using bark from local oak trees. The town still possesses several of the pubs that kept the wool and leather workers entertained. Curiously, most of them seem to be haunted, usually by female figures. The King's Arms has the strangest ghost, that of a young lady who, while waiting for her boyfriend, fell into an ancient well-shaft which suddenly opened up beneath her – falling down while being stood up perhaps.

To the east of the town is the terminal station of the South Devon Railway, the Old Dart Valley Railway, closed in 1962 but restored by enthusiasts. The line formerly linked Ashburton with Totnes, but the Ashburton to Buckfastleigh section was lost forever when the A38 trunk road took its course. Now steam engines pull trains from Buckfastleigh to Totnes and back, following the Dart for one of Britain's prettiest rides. There is a small railway museum at Buckfastleigh station.

Close to the station is Buckfast Butterflies and the Dartmoor Otter Sanctuary. Here a tropical rain forest has been recreated within which a number of typical butterfly species breed. There are also terrapins and some rain forest birds. The otter sanctuary is an outside area where otters are bred.

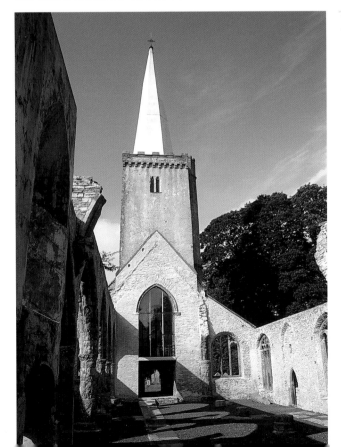

The burnt-out ruins of Holy Trinity Church

e Walk down through the town to reach a T-junction. Turn left along Church Street and you will shortly encounter the Relief Road. Turn left, passing the plaque commemorating the opening of the road on your left-hand side. Across the road there is a footpath, unsignposted, which climbs up the bank doubling back on itself. This goes up to a no-through road which leads up to Holy Trinity Church.

C Holy Trinity Church

The church was built in the 13th century, its hill top position – well away from the town – explained by a local legend that all attempts to build closer to the town were frustrated by the Devil stealing the stones each night and depositing them on the hill. This is a curious story, at odds with the usual form of the legend where a heavenly agency shifts the stones, favouring a holier site. The remoteness of the church meant that in the 1980s the building and churchyard became a focus for louts and on 21 July 1992 an arson attack resulted in the church being almost completely destroyed. Local stories circulated that the fire was the work of Satanists, perhaps bolstered by the legend of the building and the nearby tomb of Richard Cabell. After the fire, services transferred to St Luke's in the town: it is unlikely that Holy Trinity will be rebuilt.

Buckfast Abbey from near Buckfastleigh

f Go through the fine lych gate and follow the path towards the church ruins. To the right, opposite the church, is the bus-shelter-like tomb of Richard Cabell.

D Squire Richard Cabell

The tomb is said to be that of Richard Cabell, the lord of the manor in the 17th century who is claimed to have been a very evil man. He is said to have bred a pack of monstrous, ferocious dogs – in some stories they were supernatural – with which he hunted the moor, not being particularly bothered whether his quarry was fox, deer or one of his tenants, and that he exercised *droit de seigneur* over his tenants' daughters. On his death in 1677 the locals erected the tomb, with its heavy top slab and iron grille, to prevent his spirit from haunting the neighbourhood. Local children maintain that if you run around the tomb to awaken his spirit and then poke your fingers through the grille Cabell will bite them. It is usually claimed that the story of the evil squire and his huge dogs inspired Conan Doyle to write *The Hound of the Baskervilles*, but as with the rest of the Cabell legend this seems to be at odds with the facts. The real Squire Richard does not seem to have been particularly wicked; his death seems to post-date the erection of the tomb, which is likely to be just the Cabell family tomb; and the stories of the squire's dogs and general wickedness seem to have arisen after Conan Doyle's book was published.

E Buckfastleigh Caves

The hill on which the church stands is composed of carboniferous limestone, Dartmoor's granite mass rising further to the west. The limestone is soluble in rainwater (a dilute acid due to dissolved carbon dioxide), caves being formed by the rainwater percolating along fault lines in the rock. The quarrying on the northern side of the hill has broken into several caves from which the bones of prehistoric animals have been excavated. One cave, known as Reed's after Edgar Reed who first explored it, has a flowstone boss (formed when a stalagmite and stalactite joined) in the shape of a man, complete with arms and head. As the boss stands almost directly below Richard Cabell's tomb, this discovery fuelled the local stories of the evil squire.

g Follow the path down through the churchyard. Soon you reach a junction with signposts on the left and right; take the path on the left. When you get to the road turn left. Continue along the road, but where it turns sharp left, go under the arch ahead – part of the abbey's medieval south gate – to return to the start.

DARTMEET

Dartmeet, the confluence of the East and West Dart Rivers, is, perhaps, the most romantic spot on the moor – the place where the united river which names the moor is born. This fine, adventurous walk starts from the confluence and climbs an excellent viewpoint.

MAPS:
Harvey Dartmoor South; OS Landranger Sheets 191, 202; OS Outdoor Leisure Sheet 28

START/FINISH:
At 672732, the car park belong ing to the Badger's Holt Café beside the bridge at Dartmeet. DevonBus 172 stops at Dartmeet

DISTANCE/ASCENT:
3 miles (4.5km)/450ft (140m)

APPROXIMATE TIME:
1½ hours

HIGHEST POINT:
Combestone Tor 1,168ft (356m)

REFRESHMENTS:
There is usually an ice cream/drinks van in the car park. The inn at Two Bridges is 6 miles (10km) to the west along the B3357

ADVICE:
The walk involves the use of three sets of stepping stones. If the river is within a few inches of the top of those at Dartmeet, come back on a drier day as those at Week Ford will almost certainly be under water. A compass and the ability to use it is important in bad visibility

The road bridge over the East Dart River at Dartmeet

Dartmeet from Combestone Tor

A Dartmeet

On the two Dart Rivers, just 100 yards (91m) or so of their confluence, there is a full complement of man-made river crossings, spanning the centuries of human occupation of the moor. In earliest times the West Dart River would have been forded, but later the stepping stones would have been added to keep travellers dry in all but the wettest weather. The clapper bridge over the East Dart River came after the stones. Dartmeet's clapper was a fine one, but needed rebuilding several times after demolition by floods. The last time is claimed to have been on 4 August 1826 when a flash flood of the East Dart brought trees and rocks which created a temporary dam when they wedged against the clapper piers. When the 'dam' collapsed the top slab and piers were washed away. Now only sections of the clapper remain. The bridge beside it was built in 1792, completing the transition from ford to road bridge.

a From the car park, go back to the road and turn right over the bridge. On the left there is a signposted path, go through the gate until you reach a signpost. To the right from here is our return route: bear left to reach the stepping stones over the West Dart River.

Cross the stones and follow the signed path southwards. The confluence of the two Darts is to the left from here: it is ironic that few visitors to Dartmeet actually see the 'meet' – but then neither do we.

The path traverses a beautiful area of rocks and trees to reach a wall gap, then veering south-south-west, follows a wall (on your left), going through another gap and passing

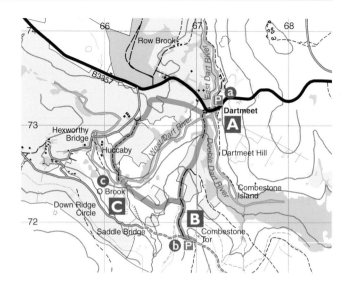

Combestone Farm and another path, to the left. Continue beside the wall, going through a gate by a shed. Here the guiding wall ends: bear half left along a track to reach a gate on to open moor. Now climb to Combestone Tor (670718), the obvious peak ahead. There is a tarmac path (with a bridge over the leat) which can be followed.

B Combestone Tor

The Tor – close to which is a car park, an alternative start for the walk – is an impressive viewpoint, both of the northern moor and Holne Moor, the wilderness to the south. Holne Moor is one of Dartmoor's best preserved prehistoric landscapes, the remains of many hut circles and cairns having been discovered, as well as a stone row and a ring cairn. The moor, and the area immediately surrounding the tor, is also criss-crossed with reaves – prehistoric field walls. To the east of the tor, close to Venford Reservoir (where there is a second car park) the ancient reave system is overlaid with medieval field boundaries.

b   After enjoying the view, return to the moor gate (668722), go through and follow a sign post marked 'Huccaby-middle path' to the west through another gate. Continue straight ahead downhill along a goodish path for 150 yards (137m), bear right at the bottom along an old wall to a very boggy area with a fence on the left. Keep going until you reach the river and gate to stepping stones across O Brook, shortly before its confluence with the West Dart.

Week Ford stepping stones

Please note: time taken calculated according to the Naismith Formula (see p.2).

C O Brook

The brook has the distinction of possessing the shortest name of any British waterway. The name is believed to derive from the Saxon for crooked. Near to where the brook reaches the West Dart (a couple of hundred yards south of Week Ford) are the remains of two tin blowing houses (see Note to Walk 24). The houses were powered by 10ft (3m) waterwheels. Mould stones for the production of tin ingots can still be seen at the rowan-shrouded ruins.

c Continue along the bank of the West Dart, reaching the Week Ford stepping stones about 100 yards (91m) from O Brook. Cross the stones and follow a path north which soon (662724) becomes a wall-enclosed lane. When the left wall bears away, follow the right wall, soon reaching another wall-enclosed lane. Follow this lane to a gate and farm. Go through the gate, then past farm buildings and bear right through another gate. Now follow a line of posts east-north-east across a field to reach a gate on to an enclosed lane. Follow the lane, crossing a stile and continuing downhill to reach a ruined building on the right. Go through the gate opposite (i.e. on your left) and follow waymarking posts (through a boggy area) to arrive at the signpost reached early in the walk. Now reverse the outward walk back to the start.

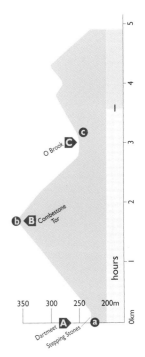

THE DEWERSTONE

MAPS:
Part on Harvey Dartmoor South, OS Landranger Sheet 201, OS Outdoor Leisure Sheet 28

START/FINISH:
At 534636, the car park beside Shaugh Bridge which crosses the River Plym to the west of Shaugh Prior. There is an alternative start at Cadover Bridge about half-way along the walk

DevonBuses 58 and 59 stop at Shaugh Prior. DevonBus 155 stops at Cadover Bridge. This bus runs only on Sundays and Public Holidays.

DISTANCE/ASCENT:
4½ miles (7km)/550ft (170m)

APPROXIMATE TIME:
3 hours

HIGHEST POINT:
820ft (250m) on the flank of Wigford Down

REFRESHMENTS:
There is an inn at Shaugh Prior a short distance to the east

ADVICE:
A good varied walk, with beautiful woodland, a short section of moorland and an excellent viewpoint. The walking is never difficult and the climbs are reasonably gentle

At the south-western extremity of the National Park, within just a few miles of the centre of Plymouth, and closer still to its airport, lies a beautiful wooded section of the River Plym's Valley. A walk along it passes close to the Dewerstone, renowned in Dartmoor mythology, and to a vast works which uses another of the moor's mineral resources – china clay.

A Shaugh Bridge

The bridge crosses the Plym just downstream of its confluence with the River Meavy and in wet weather offers a marvellous view of thrashing water. In January 1823 heavy rain, combined with the thawing of moorland snow, caused the river to rise rapidly and the bridge was destroyed. The present bridge is a replacement built a few years later. The bridge is often associated with NT Carrington, the 'Dartmoor Poet' who drew much of his inspiration from the view. Carrington is remembered in graffiti at the Dewerstone (see below).

a Near the entrance to the car park there are steps beside the ruins of the china clay drying kilns. Climb these and follow the path at the top east to reach a path junction. There, turn left along a path signed for Cadover Bridge. This path is now followed all the way to the bridge. The path is known as the

The Dewerstone

Pipe Track as it follows the line of an underground pipe which carried china clay from Cadover Bridge to the Shaugh Bridge drying kilns: in a few places sections of the old pipe can be seen breaking through the surface. It is a fine path, sometimes just inside the Plym Valley woodland, sometimes outside. When the path is above the woodland there are fine views across the valley to the Dewerstone and, later, Wigford Down.

The sylvan beauty of the woods near the Dewerstone

After an open section of walking north-east on the flank of West Down the path reaches a wall. Cross this by way of a stile to reach a path through North Wood, another beautiful section of mixed woodland. Several more stiles are crossed before the path reaches a road opposite the Shaugh Lake China Clay Works.

B   China Clay

Granite is an igneous rock formed from molten magma reaching the surface from deep within the earth. The speed of cooling of the magma defines the size of the crystals of

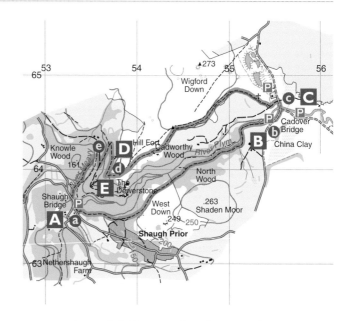

quartz, mica and feldspar within the rock. Coarse-grained rock, in which the crystals are large, has more and deeper fissures allowing water to penetrate deep into the rock. The water attacks feldspar crystals forming hydrous silicates of aluminium and potassium. Well below the surface this process is assisted by gases rising from deep within the earth. The decomposed feldspar forms a powder which, in its purest form is called kaolin after *Kao Lin* mountain in China where the fine clay was first worked. Kaolin – china clay – is used to create the finest porcelain.

It is claimed that the south-west's china clay industry started in the mid-18th century when William Cookworthy, a Quaker from Kingsbridge, a town on the Devon coast, to the south of the National Park, realised the potential of the kaolin deposits when he was visiting Hensbarrow, near Bodmin. The Cornish tin industry was in decline so there was no shortage of workers when Cookworthy decided to dig the clay. He opened a factory in Plymouth and there, in 1768, he produced the first genuine English porcelain.

Not until 1830 was it realised that Dartmoor also had deposits of kaolin, though these lie only on the southern edge of the moor. Only the deposits on Lee Moor, to the east of Shaugh Prior were found to be commercially viable: by the mid-19th century there were several mines on the moor. The kaolin is exposed by tearing away the top surface of the moor and is then either dug out and transferred to settling tanks, or washed into tanks by water sprays. In the first settling tank the heavy quartz and mica particles sink to the bottom, the purer clay solution being drawn off into another tank. In the second tank the clay particles settle out, water being drawn off and the 'mud' residue being kiln-dried to produce pure kaolin. Once the clay was used almost exclusively in the making of porcelain, but today that is only a minor usage, over 80 per cent being used in the production of paper. Other uses include textiles and cosmetics.

One of the interesting aspects of the Dartmoor industry was the use of water as a transport medium. To make the best use of their plant, the owners needed to bring the clay to the site cheaply and efficiently; with Dartmoor's relative abundance of water this was achieved by using gravity to transfer the clay in solution through pipes such as that followed by the walk.

b Turn left (N) along the road, soon reaching Cadover Bridge (555646).

C Cadover Bridge

There has been a bridge over the Plym here since at least 1291 when the 'ponte de Cada worth' was mentioned in a charter. The meaning of the name is unclear. Cad meant 'battle' in Celtic (explaining its frequent use as a prefix in Celtic leader names – Cadwalladr, for example) and some have suggested a battle at this point on the river. But there are a number of other Celtic (Welsh) words also starting with cad which do not derive from battle sites and so the true meaning is obscure. From the bridge there is a good view of the spoil heaps of the china clay works and the moor beyond.

c Cross the bridge and turn left along a track west-south-west (not the farm track to Cadworthy Farm), soon reaching a medieval cross which had fallen and been buried in windblown soil, but was found during a military exercise in 1873. The cross was then restored and re-erected. Beyond the cross the walk follows the boundary wall on the left, climbing on to the flank of Wigford Down and contouring around its southern edge. The Down has several Bronze Age remains near its summit, these including two cairn circles, several hut circles and an enclosure. The wall eventually turns left: the path follows it, going gently downhill, then bears away right by the edge of Cadworthy Wood. After about 250 yards (230m) the path crosses the ramparts of an Iron Age hillfort.

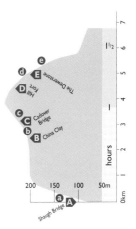

Please note: time taken calculated according to the Naismith Formula (see p.2)

D Hillfort

There are so many Neolithic and Bronze Age remains on the moor that it comes as a surprise to discover a feature as new as the Iron Age. Iron-using folk crossed to Britain in the first millennium BC. These were the ancestors of the Celts who fought the Romans and, later, the Saxons before being pushed into their strongholds of Wales and Cornwall. They were a belligerent, tribal folk, their most enduring mark on the English landscape being their hillforts. Usually these were constructed at the tops of hills, ramparts and ditches being added to the natural defensive barrier to resist attack by other tribes. Here, in the Plym Valley, the Celts built a different kind of defence, a promontory fort in which a natural triangular spur of land, defended on the south by the cliffs of the Plym Valley – including the Dewerstone – and on the west by the steep Meavy Valley was protected on the third side by a constructed rampart and ditch.

d Beyond the ramparts, continue along the path to reach the top of the Dewerstone (538638).

E The Dewerstone

Dewer is said to be a local name for the Devil and in legend he and his hounds chased sinners across the moor causing them to throw themselves off the rock in terror so he could collect their souls at the base. One particularly gruesome tale relates that an old farmer wending his weary way home met the Devil carrying a sack away from the base of the rock. In failing light and with failing eyesight the farmer did not recognise the Devil and, assuming he was a hunter, asked whether he had had a successful day. The Devil laughed and thrust the bag at the former telling him he was welcome to the catch. The gleeful old man hurried home and called to his wife to come and see what he had got. When the pair emptied the sack it contained the broken body of their son.

Coupled with such a dreadful, yet fascinating, tale few would doubt that the tree-shrouded Dewerstone, a sinister place in failing light with a teeth-chattering wind blowing, was the haunt of the Devil, but it is worth noting that some believe the name actually derives from nothing more alarming than 'dove rock'.

From the rock there is a fine view across the Plym Valley. On clear days Plymouth Breakwater can be seen. The closer view reveals several inscriptions (mostly 19th century graffiti) including one to NT Carrington, the Dartmoor poet. There was a plan to erect a memorial to him on the spot he loved so much, but the plan failed, only the inscription with the date of his death (in September 1830 at the age of 53: he is buried near Bath) being completed.

Dewerstone is now a very popular rock climbing site and walkers are likely to see climbers in action. In 1960 one climber found a Bronze Age drinking vessel wedged into a crevice in the rock.

e From the Dewerstone the path bears north through the fine Dewerstone Wood to reach a disused quarry. A search of the woodland here reveals several items of 19th century quarry equipment. Just beyond the quarry the path turns sharp left. Bear left, going behind a house and continuing down a narrow path towards the River Meavy. Continue with the river on your left, soon reaching the Meavy/Plym confluence at Shaugh Bridge. Cross the footbridge over the Plym to regain the start.

The River Plym near Cadover Bridge

SHARP TOR AND CRAZY WELL POOL

MAPS:
Harvey Dartmoor South, OS Landranger Sheet 202, OS Outdoor Leisure Sheet 28

START/FINISH:
There are several car parks beside the B3212 below Sharp Tor. The best is that at 557706, near the high point of road

DevonBus 82, which links Plymouth with Totnes via Princetown and Moretonhampstead, stops at the Sharp Tor car park

DISTANCE/ASCENT:
4¾ miles (7.5km)/550ft (170m)

APPROXIMATE TIME:
3¼ hours

HIGHEST POINT:
Sharp Tor 1,328ft (405m)

REFRESHMENTS:
None on the route, but available at Dousland and Yelverton, to the west along the B3212 and at Princetown to the east along the same road

ADVICE:
A straightforward walk, but with a wild moorland feel on the first and final stretches. The Devonport Leat cascade needs care when descending as it is steep with loose boulders

This lovely little walk on the moor to the north of Burrator Reservoir and just a short distance from Yelverton, has everything – a couple of splendid tors, fine views, a short section of forest walking, prehistoric ruins and a pool steeped in legend.

a From the car park head south-east straight up Sharp Tor (marked as Sharpitor on the OS maps: there are inconsistencies in other local spellings too, Leather Tor is Lether Tor and Peek Hill is Peak Hill in the writings of old moormen). This is a fine tor, offering a superb view south over Burrator Reservoir to Sheeps Tor, and east over the southern moor.

After admiring the view, head south-east, following a wall to the northern end of Leather Tor. Now make your way through the summit clitter and descend southwards at any convenient point to reach a track at the forest edge (565696). Turn left

Ice-covered Crazy Well Pool – a flooded tinwork

and follow the track, soon crossing a new clapper-style bridge over the Devonport Leat (see Note to Walk 23). Continue along the track into the forest. As noted elsewhere (see Note to Walk 23) the forest is now home to crossbills. The track winds easily NE through the forest, descending gently to cross Leather Tor Bridge (569699) over the River Meavy.

A   Leather Tor Bridge

The bridge is a clapper dating from 1833 when it replaced the stepping stones known as Reddipit Steps. Just before reaching the bridge, to the left of the track, there are two caves excavated into the granite. These are fogous, storage caves for farm produce. Potatoes were often stored in such caves as they could be kept dark and frost free and, therefore, preserved over long periods. To ensure darkness and to keep out the cold potato caves would be fitted with doors, this requiring elaborate door jambs and lintels. The potato cave here is 35ft (10m) deep.

b   Continue eastwards to reach a prominent track junction close to the forest edge. Here the main rutted track (Raddick Lane) bears left, but our route goes ahead (E), then left at a T-junction of tracks to emerge from the forest. Follow the

Leather Tor

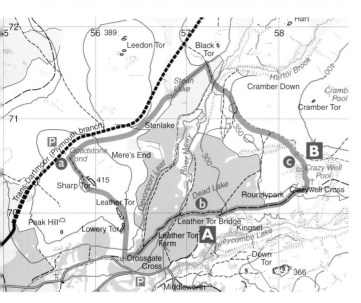

track, with the forest to your left and a fine view to Down Tor on your right. In the valley below the tor (of the Newleycombe Lake stream) are the ruins of old tin mines.

Go through a gate on to open moor, continuing along the track until a stream crosses it on its way down to Newleycombe Lake. Here, turn left and follow the stream uphill to reach Crazy Well Pool (582705).

B Crazy Well Pool

The pool is not natural, but a spring-filled hollow created by medieval tin miners. Legend has it that it is bottomless, a legend supported by a story that the village folk of Walkhampton, to the west, in whose parish the pool lies, tied the church bell-ropes together and lowered them into the water to try to plumb the depth. They failed, confirming, in their own minds at least, the bottomless theory. In fact, the pool is about 15ft (5m) deep.

Much more sinister is the story that the pool is prophetic. This tale seems to derive from a curious incident relating to Piers Gaveston, favourite (and probably lover) of Edward II and Warden of the Royal Forest of Dartmoor. Exiled from the court when the nobility threatened rebellion if Edward allowed him to stay, Gaveston is said to have sought refuge on Dartmoor and visited the pool. This is an immediate problem as the tin miners' activities which created Crazy Well post-date

Please note: time taken calculated according to the Naismith Formula (see p.2)

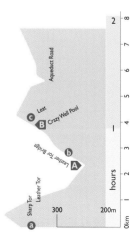

Gaveston's time – was there a natural pool here before the miners came?

One version of Gaveston's story claims that he deliberately visited the pool, knowing of its prophetic talent, but another claims that he had a chance meeting with a witch who lived on Sheeps Tor. Whichever is the case, Gaveston was told his future in a riddle which he interpreted incorrectly. He returned to Court, the nobility did indeed rise in rebellion and Gaveston was captured at Scarborough after the castle had been besieged by soldiers of the Earl of Pembroke. Gaveston was taken south towards the Earl's castle at Wallingford in Oxfordshire, but as they neared the castle the Earl rode ahead and Gaveston was seized by the Earl of Warwick who had him hanged on Blacklow Hill. Gaveston's misreading of the prophecy had been fatal.

This strange story led to a local tale that the pool prophesied death, and that each evening it spoke the name of the next person to die in Walkhampton parish. So fearful of hearing their own name were the locals that no one would approach the pool at dusk or during the night. It was also said that on Midsummer's Eve the face of the next person in the parish to die could be seen in the pool. As has often been noted, this is a strange story as anyone peering into the pool was likely to see their own reflection. But within living memory two local lads went to stare into the pool one Midsummer's Eve. They had been drinking and had more beer with them, and so should not have been on the motorcycle on which they drove home in the dark. It left the road and they were both killed. It was an unnecessary tragedy of course – but it is certainly the case that they were the last two faces reflected in the pool.

A short distance east of the pool is a fine medieval cross (called Clazywell Cross in many old books, there having long been confusion over the name of the pool and cross: confusion made even more so by giving one name to each) marking a path which crossed the southern moor to Siward's Cross (see Note to Walk 22).

c   From the pool head north, uphill, to reach the Devonport Leat, where it is marginally easier to walk along the right bank. Turn left (NE) and follow the channel around Raddick Hill. At one point the leat performs a neat, tight half-circle to hold the contour, then descends in a fine cascade to reach an aqueduct over the River Meavy (573714). The original aqueduct was wooden, supported on the same granite piers that hold up the present channel. Cross the river and the leat (573714), then climb uphill towards the B3212, bearing left to walk beside the road – or across the moor between the forest, left, and the road, right, to return to the start.

The Devonport Leat cascading down Raddick Hill to the aqueduct over the River Meavy

22

CHILDE'S TOMB

MAPS:
Harvey Dartmoor South, OS Landranger Sheet 202, Outdoor Leisure Sheet 28

START/FINISH:
At Whiteworks (613710), a hamlet reached by a minor road from Princetown. Parking is possible at several points along this road as it approaches the hamlet and in the hamlet itself. Please park with consideration for residents and other road users.

No buses serve Whiteworks. The closest bus stop is at Princetown, which is served by several cross-moor buses.

DISTANCE/ASCENT:
5 miles (8km)/400ft (120m)

APPROXIMATE TIME:
2½ hours

HIGHEST POINT:
Crane Hill 1,545ft (471m)

REFRESHMENTS:
None on the route, but several possibilities in Princetown.

ADVICE:
Good tracks at the start are soon replaced by trackless moor which can be difficult after rain, particularly across Crane Hill. The route rounds Foxtor Mires, one of Dartmoor's most treacherous bogs – choose a good day for this walk. This is wild Dartmoor, so navigational skills are required

O f all the tales associated with Dartmoor the most famous is *The Hound of the Baskervilles* which pits Sherlock Holmes and Dr Watson against a huge phantom dog. This walk visits the mire which probably inspired the book as well as the site of one of the moor's most tragic incidents.

A   Whiteworks

The hamlet grew up around the Whiteworks tin mine, the ruins and debris of which can be seen all around the road end. To the south and north-east of the hamlet are the remains of shafts sunk to the lode-bearing rocks. Almost all Dartmoor's shafts have been capped for safety reasons – and often, as with several here at Whiteworks, they have been further protected by walls – but can often be distinguished as cone-shaped pits with a semi-circle of debris on the downhill slope (the debris on the uphill slope having fallen in on to the cap). The name of the tin mine here seems to have derived from the large amount of kaolin (see Note to Walk 20) found in the rock.

a   From Whiteworks, follow the road back towards Princetown, reaching an indistinct track to the left at 605707, at the start of a long right-hand bend. Take this track, heading south-west. After 300 yards (274m) the track crosses another heading north-south: ignore this, continuing to reach another intersecting track after a further 150 yards (137m). Here turn left (S) following the improved track to Nun's Cross Farm for Siward's Cross (605699).

B   Siward's Cross

This fine cross dates from at least 1240 when it was mentioned, as *Crucem Sywardi*, as a marker of the eastern boundary of the lands of Buckland Abbey. The name Syward, or Siward, is claimed by most experts to be from an 11th-century Dane, the Earl of Northumbria. It is curious that a Dane would hold land here in deepest Saxon-held England, but Siward, together with Leofric of Mercia, supported the Saxon king Edward the Confessor in his dispute with Earl Godwine and may have been rewarded with a piece of Wessex. Siward is an interesting man: he was married to an Angian princess and at the same time as supporting King Edward invaded Scotland, fighting against Macbeth. This is the real Macbeth, the man who really did follow Duncan (but did not murder him in the way Shakespeare describes). In Shakespeare's play Siward is portrayed as 'Old Siward'. Siward lost his son, also called Siward, in the battle against Macbeth. Good though the story is, it has to be said that some experts believe the name derives from a family called Siward who are known to have lived in Cholwich Town, to the south of the cross, in the 13th century. The cross has Siward (possibly Syward, but spellings in early medieval England were often haphazard) inscribed on one side. On the other side 'Bocland' is inscribed. As this faces Buckland Abbey it would seem to be conclusive that the cross was raised by the Abbey, but Buckland was also a local ward for free-hold land, that is land held with official deeds – 'book land', so the possibility of the cross being named for the local family remains.

To add further confusion, the cross is also referred to as Nun's Cross on OS maps and in many reference books. Despite the potential Buckland Abbey connection there were no Dartmoor nuns so that cannot be the reason for the name. Most likely this name pre-dates both the cross and the Saxons, deriving

Siward's or Nun's Cross looking towards Nun's Cross Farm

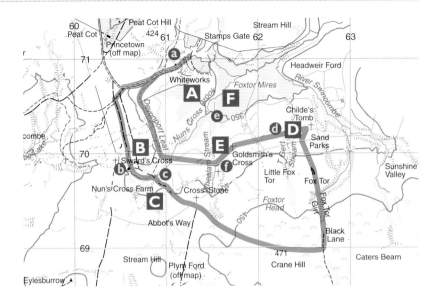

from the Celtic 'nant' which means a 'stream' or 'stream gorge', quite an apt name for a place between east and west running streams.

In 1846 the cross was pushed over by vandals, breaking about half-way along its shaft. It was repaired, with a visible iron band, by a John Newcombe, to whom all lovers of Dartmoor should be grateful.

b At the path junction (604699), ignore the tracks continuing south (towards the Eylesbarrow tin mine – see Walk 24), and head east-south-east past the ruins of Nun's Cross Farm, keeping them on your left.

C   Abbot's Way and Nun's Cross Farm

The Abbot's Way is named on maps of Dartmoor and its route can be traced across the southern moor as it heads for Buckfast Abbey. It is assumed that the route led from the Abbey to Whitchurch Priory – but there is a problem. The name seems to have been applied to the route only in the 18th century, 200 years after the Dissolution of the Monasteries, and such evidence as does exist implies that the moorland route to Buckfast actually ran further east, across Holne Moor. The evidence lies in the number of moorland crosses which mark that route: only Siward's Cross lies comfortably on the route of the supposed Abbot's Way.

But that is not to say that the 'Abbot's Way' is not a true ancient track. It is very likely that it was indeed a route, one taken by 'jobbers', men who led teams of packhorses across the moor. There is even some evidence that the route was originally called the Jobber's Path. It is also possible that the jobbers occasionally carried wool to and from the Buckfast estates – so Abbot's Way may not be such a bad name after all.

The ruin of Nun's Cross Farm is a reminder of how harsh Dartmoor can be to those who try to tame it, but is also a reminder of a tale that exemplifies the spirit of Dartmoor folk. A traveller, caught in a dreadful storm with lashing rain and ferocious wind, sought shelter in an old farm. Inside he and the farmer stood against the wall as rain poured through the roof. In exasperation the traveller asked the farmer why he did not mend the roof. What? said the farmer, only an idiot would mend a roof on a day like this. Even more exasperated the traveller asked why the farmer did not mend the roof on a fine day. What? said the farmer, waste good weather and time fixing a roof that's not giving trouble.

c Follow the track (part of the Abbot's Way) south-eastwards from the farm, and at the sluice gate on the leat, turn right (608697) and head uphill on the occasionally indistinct moorland track towards Crane Hill. The way passes near Cross Stone (613695), and shortly (at 615692) veers sharply south-west (heading towards Plym Ford where the infant River Plym is crossed): maintain direction towards Crane Hill. From the top (622690), head east over boggy ground to reach the Black Lane peat pass (at 627690), its southern end marked by a post, one of several that bring a route from the southern moor to Fox Tor. Follow the pass north and walk through the tin mine debris in Fox Tor Girt before climbing to the shallow summit and twin tors of Fox Tor (626698).

From the tors, head north, descending to reach a gate (625701) in the east-west running wall. Go through and maintain direction, soon reaching a cross mounted on a broad stone cairn. This is Childe's Tomb (624702).

D Childe's Tomb

The cairn is probably Bronze Age, though may have been modified later. The cross is certainly medieval, perhaps even Saxon, its true age being dependent on the real age of one of Dartmoor's most tragic tales. It involves a man who owned land near Plymstock and who was out hunting on the moor one cold winter's day. He was a good hunter and on this day

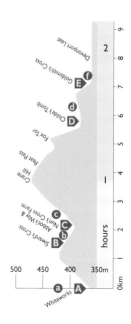

rode away from his colleagues in his pursuit of quarry. He was also a strong man so the fact that he was alone in late afternoon did not bother him. But a storm blew up suddenly, the wind scything across the moor and snow falling thickly. The man became hopelessly lost and soon realised his life was in danger. Eventually, overcome by cold and fear, he killed his horse, slitting it open and crawling inside to gain warmth and protection from the wind. The warmth was, of course, short-lived. The man's clothes were soaked with the horse's blood and froze into an icy plating around him. By morning he was dead.

Childe's Tomb and Fox Tor on a midsummer evening

There are a couple of versions about what happened next. One insists that the man had made a will giving all his land to the church in which he was buried. Another version has it that he wrote this request in horse's blood on a boulder near his last resting place. (There is also a version that has him writing the message in blood on the snow, but that seems nonsense.) Whichever is the case, the lands were a significant prize, and the man's loss on the moor persuaded the monks of Tavistock out on to the moor as soon as the storm cleared. They found the body and started to carry it back to their abbey. Hearing this the Plymstock folk set out to ambush the monks, intent on stealing the body for their own church and capturing the spoils. The Plymstock folk prepared an ambush at the bridge over the River Tavy that the Tavistock monks would have to cross. But the monks were tipped off about the ambush and hastily built a temporary bridge over the river. Crossing this they rushed to the abbey and completed the burial before the enraged Plymstock men arrived, completing an undignified end to a tragic tale.

The temporary bridge built by the Tavistock monks is now called Guile Bridge which would tie in with the story nicely but for experts maintaining that 'guile' is actually a corruption of 'guild' because the bridge was built by the Tavistock guilds. The name of the site represents another mystery. One version of the story places it in the early medieval period and calls the hunter Amos (or Amys) Childe, but another version pushes the tale back to the 11th century and maintains the hunter was a Saxon called Ordulf. If the latter was true then the name would be from 'cild', the Saxon for 'leader'. But why tomb, since the hunter was clearly buried at Tavistock? Possibly because winter made the immediate transport of the body off the moor impossible, requiring a temporary burial on the moor.

d   From Childe's Tomb, contour well to the south of Foxtor Mires heading west-south-west for about ½ mile (400m), to a cross mounted on a boulder (616702). In fog use the gated wall by which you entered as a guide, continuing direct to the leat (see para f).

E   Goldsmith's Cross

The cross is named for Lt Goldsmith RN who was responsible for re-erecting it after it had lain flat for many years. Goldsmith made a habit of re-erecting crosses in Devon and Cornwall, a personal crusade after he had been responsible for the destruction of Cornwall's most famous logan rock at Treen. (For an explanation of logan rocks see Note to Walk

14.) The locals at Treen had claimed that the rock could not be toppled, but Goldsmith, together with a few of his men and an assortment of levers and other equipment, had proved them wrong. The locals were appalled, as were Goldsmith's Royal Navy superiors who ordered him to restore the logan to its original position – at his own expense. This he did, though sadly the logan no longer rocked.

e   Do not attempt to cross Foxtor Mires. Some maps show a bridleway across the mires but this route does not exist and should not be attempted under any circumstances.

F   Foxtor Mires

The Note to Walk 10 explains that there are two forms of bog on Dartmoor, upland (or blanket) and valley bog. Foxtor Mires are among the very best examples of the latter. Valley or mire bogs form where slow-moving rivers allow the valley bottoms to become waterlogged. Although the waterlogged acidic soil is not attractive to many plants – though at the fringes lesser spearwort, bog pimpernel, bog asphodel and the insectivorous sundew can occasionally be seen – it has enough nutrients to allow sphagnum moss to grow in abundance. Sphagnum is an interesting moss, used as a field dressing during the 1914–18 War and as an early form of nappy because of its amazing potential to absorb fluids and its mild antiseptic qualities. It is usually seen as an insipid yellow base in hanging baskets, but in valley bogs it is bright green, making the bogs seem attractive oases in a desert of bleak moor. Do not be deceived, the entire surface is fluid, leading to other names for valley bogs – featherbeds or quakers. They can support the weight of a walker, but can also allow the same walker to sink knee or thigh deep and to be left floundering. One famous Dartmoor tale has it that a man walking beside a valley bog noticed a top hat sat on the sphagnum. Gingerly he crossed to it and lifted it up. To his astonishment there was a head underneath, its owner asking for assistance in being freed from the bog. When the rescuer asked what he should attach the hauling rope to, the now-hatless man suggested it would be best fastened to the horse he was sat on. Stories of men being drowned in valley bogs are probably exaggerations, although some experts believe that ponies may well be engulfed occasionally, their long legs being very poorly designed for extricating them, particularly if they fall on their sides. But do not allow the fact that valley bogs are unlikely to kill you make you complacent – being trapped in one could be a very nasty experience.

It is likely that the reputation of valley bogs led Sir Arthur Conan Doyle to set *The Hound of the Baskervilles* on Dartmoor. Some of the book's locations are obvious moor features, but others are not as exact. Despite this, most Sherlock Holmes enthusiasts believe Conan Doyle set Baskerville Hall near Whiteworks, with Foxtor Mires being the model for Grimpen Mire and Fox Tor the book's High Tor. If your trip is in failing light it would be easy to gaze across Foxtor Mire and believe the wind through the Fox tors was the howling of a giant dog.

A view over Whiteworks Tin Mine and Fox Tor Mire

f From Goldsmith's Cross, return to the wall to the south, turn right and follow it west-south-west to reach the Devonport Leat (at about 609699). Turn right again and follow the leat north-north-west until it meets the road about 600 yards (550m) west of Whiteworks. Follow the road back to the start.

BURRATOR RESERVOIR

MAPS:
Harvey Dartmoor South, OS
Landranger Sheets 201 and
202, OS Outdoor Leisure Sheet
28

START/FINISH:
At 568694, the car park at the
eastern end of Burrator
Reservoir. There is a second car
park close to western of the
two dams of the reservoir's
southern end which also lies
on the route

DevonBus 48 links Wembury to
Burrator. The bus runs only on
Sundays and Public Holidays

DISTANCE/ASCENT:
6 miles (9.5km)/450ft (140m)

APPROXIMATE TIME:
3½ hours

HIGHEST POINT:
Sheeps Tor 1,211ft (369m)

REFRESHMENTS:
There is an inn at Meavy, and
in summer there are often ice
cream vans in the car parks

ADVICE:
A very easy, straightforward
walk

Dartmoor averages about 60in (1.52m) of rain annually,
the moor's western edge receiving closer to 100in
(2.54m) as it faces the prevailing Atlantic weather. As
early as the 16th century this water was seen as a valuable
resource and channelled off the moor. Then, in 1898, the first (of
several) reservoirs was created at Burrator. This excellent walk
circumnavigates the reservoir, visiting two delightful hamlets
and a fine tor.

a   From Norsworthy Bridge follow the road south-west for a
few yards before turning right (567694) over a stile into a
plantation. Continue northwards and then north-west,
crossing another stile and a minor road, to a junction with a
cross path along the Devonport Leat (565697). Here turn left
and follow the southern bank of the leat until you reach a
junction with a road. Here turn right and go a few metres
north-west to Cross Gate (561695). From Cross Gate follow
the path westwards (north of the road and leat), crossing a
stile and then a minor road (553692). The path continues in
a southerly direction through a plantation and follows the line
of the leat to a road crossing (551688). The track opposite
joins the old rail track. Turn left here and follow the path
southwards.

The path enters open moorland at Yennadon Down (550686).
From here follow the western side of the woods. Continue
southwards and take the track down to the road just south of
the western dam of the Burrator Reservoir.

A   Burrator Reservoir

As early as the 1560s it was proposed to cut a leat from
Dartmoor to Plymouth, supplying drinking water to the town,
but it was not until an Act of Parliament in 1585 that the city
was finally authorised to 'digge a Trench throughe and over all
the landes and groundes lying between Plymouth and anye
parts of the said river of Mew'. The river was, of course, the
Meavy. Despite the Act, it was a further five years before Sir
Francis Drake finally got the project underway by digging the
first turf. The local tin miners were consulted, perhaps even
employed, and an 18-mile (29km) leat was constructed from
the Meavy to the west of Sheepstor village to Plymouth. The
leat, begun in December 1590, was completed in April 1591,

having been cut at the astonishing rate of 1 mile (1.6km) per week. It is often claimed that the leat was the greatest of all Tudor engineering feats. The leat provided water to the town for more than 300 years until it was replaced by a supply from the Burrator reservoir. The leat is now disused.

Two centuries after the completion of what is still known as Drake's Leat there was a need for an enhanced water supply. Devonport, the naval dockyard, and the town that grew up around it had developed a significant thirst, but Plymouth, which saw itself in competition with the new town, was reluctant to satisfy the thirst from its own supply. Samuel Johnson, visiting Plymouth in 1762, speaking of the inhabitants of Devonport, put it succinctly – 'Let them die of thirst, they shall not have a drop'. Hardly the most charitable of attitudes. It seems to have prevailed though, at least in part, as in 1793 a new leat was dug. This was a much longer

The village cross and ancient oak tree on the green at Meavy

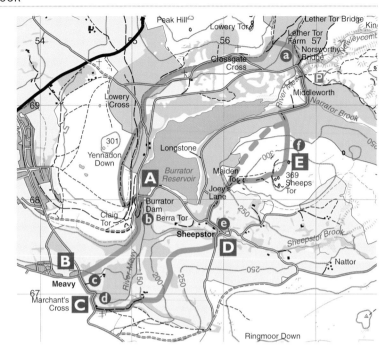

channel taking water from the West Dart to the north-east of Burrator. From close to the reservoir's southern end the two leats (Drake's and what is now called Devonport Leat, though it was originally the Dock Leat) run very close together. From Dousland the Devonport Leat was channelled to the town.

In 1898 the upper Meavy Valley was dammed to produce the Burrator Reservoir to supply the growing needs of Plymouth/Devonport. Initially the reservoir had a capacity of 650 million gallons (about 4.5 thousand million litres) in 1928. The dam that holds back the water is faced with 6 ton granite blocks.

Burrator means 'wooded tor' an apt name since the planting of the trees around the reservoir. Many of these are alien pine species raising the old debate about the acceptability of reservoirs and commercial forestry in a National Park. In the case of Burrator both water and trees actually pre-date the creation of the park, and do add an extra dimension to the area. The combination of forest (some of them now mixed) and water is visually very attractive, and has brought new bird species to the area. The crossbill nests in the forest and goshawks are occasionally seen.

b Just beyond the western dam, go through the gate beside the toilets, turn left and go downhill along a path that soon reaches the, now dry, Drake's Leat (see Note above). The path now follows the leat – there are also yellow waymarkers – then leaves it to go through a fine section of woodland before emerging in open country with small clumps of oak trees. Follow the path across a lane and continue to reach a minor road (at 544672). The lane opposite and slightly left can be followed for a short detour into Meavy.

B Meavy

The detour into Meavy passes, to the left, the village school which displays a replica of Drake's Drum. As the plaque notes, this was originally used to summon village children to the school. Further on is the village green with the old cross and a very old (and somewhat battered) oak tree. It has been suggested that the tree is as old as the church, but that would make it at least 700 years old as the church has 13th century origins (and maybe even older). The church tower is 15th century. The village's old Church House – often called church ale houses as they were brewhouses as well as meeting houses (see Note to Walk 17).

c Our walk does not go through Meavy, turning left along the minor road (right if you have detoured to the village), and following it to a ford. Stepping stones offer the shortest way here, but there is a bridge for guaranteed dryness. Continue along the road to reach Marchant's Cross (546668).

C Marchant's Cross

The cross is first mentioned in a charter of 1291 when it was named as one of the boundary markers of the estate of Buckland Abbey. It was then named Smalacumbacrosse and was already ancient. It has been suggested that it was raised as a waymarker on a track from Tavistock Abbey, marking the point where this branched to South Hams and Plympton Priory. This would perhaps explain why it is at the base of Lynch Hill, rather than the usual siting at the top of a climb, though a local legend might also explain the position. The legend claims that travellers would kneel at the cross and pray for good fortune before setting out southwards across the bleak moor. There is also a story that the cross marks the grave of a suicide. This does not seem to have been the Marchant of the name as the nearby ford is also occasionally called Marchant's Ford. What is more likely is that Marchant was a local landowner.

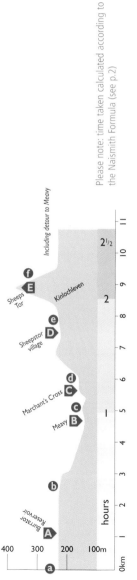

Please note: time taken calculated according to the Naismith Formula (see p.2)

Burrator Reservoir from Sheeps Tor looking towards Sharpitor and Leather Tor

d At the cross, turn left and follow the lane east to Yeo Farm, dated 1610 above the porch. Just before the old farmhouse, bear right along a track, soon turning left at a track junction. Follow the track, then path, along the edge of Burrator Wood. Follow the path into the wood, bearing right with it to emerge over a wall. Now head east-north-east crossing fields close to the hedge on the left to reach a prominent, waymarked gate. Go through and bear half-left across the field beyond to reach a lane, following it to a minor road (Portland Lane 559676) and turn left to reach Sheepstor.

D Sheepstor

This picturesque hamlet, with its dark-stoned cottages huddled around a typical moorland church, has much of interest. It began life as a tin miners' settlement, the church dating from the 16th century. Inside there is a beautiful rood screen, an exact copy from the early years of the 20th century of the medieval original. The strange carving above the church's front porch dates from the 17th century. It shows a skull, with bones in its mouth and ears of corn sprouting from its eye sockets, above an hourglass. The skull and hourglass reminded the congregation that when their time has come, death comes to everyone, but that new life springs from death. The carving would be seen by everyone as they entered the church and would reinforce the Bible's message that only by leading a good life was salvation guaranteed.

In the churchyard are the graves of three English-born Rajahs of Sarawak. James Brooke was born in Bengal in 1803, the son of a judge employed by the East India Company. In 1839 Brooke was asked by the Governor of Singapore to sail to Sarawak to present gifts and thanks to the Rajah for his kindness to a group of shipwrecked British sailors. When Brooke arrived he found the country in turmoil, pirates and rebels terrorising the population. He helped to restore peace, so successfully that the locals asked him to become the new Rajah. He accepted and remained Rajah until 1863, seeing Sarawak recognised as an independent country and being made a KCB by Queen Victoria for his efforts. He retired to Sheepstor where he died in 1868. He is, rather surprisingly, buried beneath a tomb of Aberdeen, rather than Dartmoor, granite. Brooke never married, and was to have been succeeded as Rajah by his nephew, but he, too, died in 1868. A younger nephew (Charles Anthony Johnson, who took the surname Brooke) therefore succeeded. He, in turn, was succeeded by his son Charles Vyner de Windt Brooke as the 3rd Rajah. This last Brooke Rajah died in 1963.

e   At the junction of Portland Lane with the main village road, turn left (NW), then bear right at the next junction. After 200 yards (183m), where the road bends left, take the unmarked, but obvious bridleway on the right (at 559680 beyond the small, ad hoc car park), soon reaching open moor. Now head directly uphill heading east-north-east to the summit of Sheeps Tor. To avoid the climb continue along the bridleway which will take you direct to Narrator Plantation

E   Sheeps Tor

The steep tor – some claim the name is from schittes, meaning a steep slope, rather than from the more obvious moorland sheep – offers superb views of Burrator Reservoir and Leather Tor/Sharpitor beyond and of the bleak southern moorland to the east and south. There is also much of interest on the tor itself. On the western flank are the remains of pillow mounds (see Note to Walk 5), while on the southern flank is a natural rocky hollow known as Pixies House. It is said that if you leave a gift here – preferably a new pin – the fairy folk will grant you a wish.

Sunset over Burrator Reservoir, as seen from Sheeps Tor

f   Descend the northern flank of the hill, heading for the eastern edge of the reservoir to reach a gate on to a track (567688). Follow the track through Narrator Plantation to reach a road beside the reservoir. Turn right and follow the road back to the start.

DRIZZLE COMBE AND EYLESBARROW

MAPS:
Harvey Dartmoor South, OS Landranger Sheet 202, Outdoor Leisure Sheet 28

START/FINISH:
At 578673, at the end of the road heading east from Sheepstor

DevonBus 48 links Wembury to Burrator and stops at the reservoir dam, to the west of Sheepstor. The bus runs only on Sundays and Public Holidays

DISTANCE/ASCENT:
8 miles (13km)/600ft (180m)

APPROXIMATE TIME:
4¼ hours

HIGHEST POINT:
1,440ft (440m) on the track between the Eylesbarrow mine and Siward's Cross

REFRESHMENTS:
None on the route, but there are usually ice cream vans near Burrator Reservoir and there is an inn at Meavy, to the west of Sheepstor

ADVICE:
A long, but straightforward walk, mostly on good, dry tracks. The open moor sections have reasonable waymarks – provided the weather is good. A compass and the ability to use it are important in poor visibility

Close to Burrator Reservoir are some of Dartmoor's most intriguing prehistoric sites and the some of the best remains of its tin industry. This walk links these sites in a superb walk across open moorland.

a The start lies to the east of Sheepstor village (see Note to Walk 23): follow the narrow road east up on to the moor. The make-shift car park lies at the road end. From it, jump or ford the stream and follow the broad, clear track easterly beyond, soon reaching a tree-shrouded Scout Hut to the right. Now turn right through the gate and follow the equally clear track – Edward's Path – heading south on the western (near) side of the hut. Follow the track gently uphill, passing Eastern Tor on the left, to reach Ditsworthy Warren House (584663).

A Ditsworthy Warren
The warren which named the house was the largest on Dartmoor, supplying rabbit meat to the tin miners of Meavy Pool and to local farmers (see, also, Note to Walk 5) on Pillow Mounds). The warren covered almost 250 acres (100ha) at first but was reputedly extended to cover almost 1000 acres (400ha) of moorland between Eastern and Shavercombe Tors. In the late 19th century a man cutting peat at the edge of the warren unearthed a Bronze Age dagger, presumably dropped by someone on their way to or from the Drizzlecombe sites.

b Go behind the house (once occupied by the warrener, but now a Royal Navy training centre), and follow the track heading east, then north-east towards the River Plym. The track eventually fades into the moor, but by then the standing stones of Drizzle Combe can be seen ahead (centred on 592671, although the whole area abounds in antiquities).

B Drizzle Combe
The combe's name is now firmly embedded in Dartmoor literature, printed on every map and repeated in most books. Yet it is a mistake, for this is Thrushel Combe, the skylark valley, a still appropriate name as anyone completing the walk during the breeding season of the birds will hear. In the heavily accented Devonian of the locals thrushel sounds like 'drishel' and so became 'drizzle'. A light rain may well have fallen on the early OS map maker to make the change complete.

The standing stone in Drizzle Combe is the tallest on Dartmoor

Within the combe – technically on the broad, wedge-shaped spur of land descending from Higher Hartor and separating Thrushel Combe from the Plym Valley – are some of Dartmoor's most striking standing stones. On the higher ground are the remains of hut circles and several pounds. Here, too, is a large cairn, probably raised over cremated remains.

On the slopes below the settlements are three stone rows each of specific form, the rows terminating in a burial cairn at the up-slope end and in a single standing stone at the down-slope end. The standing stones (usually termed menhirs from the Celtic maen hir – long stone) are among the tallest on the moor: indeed at 14ft (4.3m) one is actually the tallest. The longest row (the most westerly) is 160 yards (145m) long and is partially of single stones, partially a row of double stones. The other rows are of single stones. The rows are not parallel to each other, but the northern and southern rows do align with large cairns near the up-slope settlement. Near the cairned end of the longest row, but not aligned with it, is a huge cairn called the Giant's Basin. The cairn is 27 yards (24.7m) in diameter and 7.5ft (2.3m) high, one of the largest on the moor, and has three small cairns close to its western side. The name derives from the circular hollow which has formed on the cairn's broad top. In addition to these features, there are also other burial sites (they are kistvaens, stone-slab boxes for cremated remains) and a small stone circle. The site is intriguing for having the megaliths so close to the settlements, the usual pattern being to have them at some remove, perhaps to enhance their majesty or spirituality, and for being so complex – virtually all the Bronze Age memorial/ritual forms are represented.

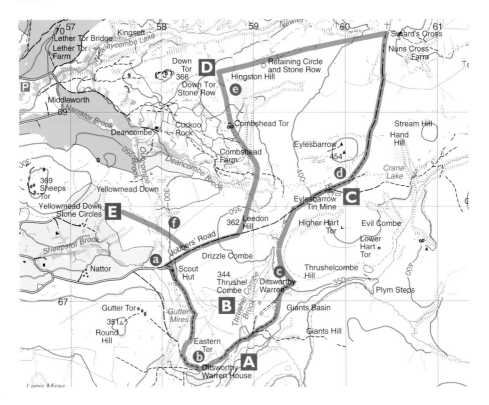

c From the megaliths head north to reach a track heading uphill north-west through Drizzle Combe. This meets the broad, clear track followed from the start to the Scout Hut. Turn right and follow the track east-north-east to the Eylesbarrow Mine (598682).

C Eylesbarrow Tin Mine

Tin is alloyed with copper to form bronze, a fact that has led some experts to consider it likely that tin was mined on Dartmoor in prehistoric times, though there is actually scant evidence for this. By early medieval times tin was being alloyed with lead to produce pewter, the main material for domestic items such as drinking cups, bowls and spoons. It was at this time that Dartmoor tin extraction became the area's most important industry: from the 12th century onwards tin mining is well documented. When the use of pewter declined, Dartmoor mining declined, but restarted when tin was again required for alloying to produce solders and for the production of plate.

The tin is present in the Dartmoor granite as tin oxide or cassiterite which occurs in concentrated places (or lodes) at various places across the moor. Where rivers cut down into a lode the cassiterite is carried away by the stream and it is likely that ore found this way was both the first used on the moor and also led to the discovery of the major lodes. The first method of extraction was by 'streaming'. Streams would be diverted, if necessary, and dammed, the breaking of the dam causing a rush of water that tore away the surface material, exposing the lode-bearing strata to view. Streaming was very destructive of the landscape, and despite the centuries since its last use (it was the preferred method of exposing a lode until the 17th century) scars from the process can still be seen in several places on the moor. Mining took over as the easiest way of obtaining cassiterite as soon as the problems of extracting water from deep shafts had been overcome.

In the early tin workings the extracted ore was smelted on site, the relatively crude moorland furnaces creating a fairly impure metal which was then carried by pack-horse to a stannary town – stannary from *stannum*, the Latin name for tin, and the basis of the metal's chemical symbol Sn – where it was re-smelted to form pure metal. Later, furnace design was improved, with waterwheels driving bellows to increase air supply and so raise temperatures. Blowing houses, as these new bellows-driven furnaces were called, are a feature of many of Dartmoor's mine ruins. Often, close to the ruins mouldstones can be found. These were large granite stones into which square holes had been chiselled. Molten metal was poured into the mouldstones to form metal ingots. The building of blowing houses on the moor reduced transport costs as only the ingots, rather than impure material had to be pack-horsed from the moor. There are the remains of two blowing houses in the Plym Valley near Plym Steps, just a short distance from Drizzle Combe.

A further refinement was the crushing of the cassiterite which made the smelting more efficient. Again a waterwheel provided the power, gearing turning its circular motion into the up-and-down movement of stamps which crushed ore between themselves and a granite mortar stone. These stones, with tell-tale circular stamp imprints, can also be found at mine sites. At some sites 'crazing' was used instead of stamping. Here two granite millstones would be used to pound the ore to a fine powder, exactly as mills grind wheat to flower. Crazing was much less popular than stamping on Dartmoor with only three crazing mill sites discovered to date.

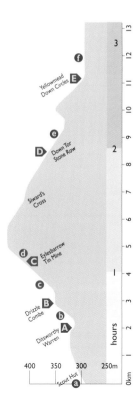

Please note: time taken calculated according to the Naismith Formula (see p.2)

The wheels which drove the bellows and stamps would have been a fine sight and it is sad that none remain. Most were about 15ft (4.5m) in diameter – the largest reached 26ft (8m) – and were fed by water from a leat dug to the site from a convenient river.

Eylesbarrow Mine was one of the later moorland ventures and was also the last active Dartmoor tin mine. Here new mining techniques were used, sinking vertical shafts into the lode and tunnelling horizontally along it, with water being extracted from the mine using water power. In addition to the mine shafts there are the remains of a dressing floor where ore was washed in 'buddles' which graded the rock so that gravel and other unwanted material could be extracted and dumped. After washing the ore was crushed in a stamp mill and then smelted. Eylesbarrow used a horizontal flue, the cooling smoke allowing tin to 'plate out' on the flue walls for later collection by scraping. While this increased the yield, it did so at the expense of the health of those carrying out the scraping who breathed air with a heavy concentration of metal and other noxious material from the flue gases.

d At the mine ruin there is a choice of routes. To the right a track goes east past the old tin miners' hostel to reach Plym Ford. Our route bears left, following the clear northerly track uphill. On top of the shallow hill on the left as you climb is the Bronze Age barrow – Eylesbarrow – which named the mine. Continue along the track, now going gently downhill to reach the ruin of Nun's Cross Farm and Siward's Cross (605699) (see Notes to Walk 22). Note that the Devonport leat is in the tunnel here. From the cross head west across fine open moor, with no easily visible paths (compass and navigation skills are essential here; avoid in bad visibility), aiming towards the old mining hummocks, then bearing left to reach a dry leat. Cross the leat and head south of west towards the obvious clutter of

Part of the ruins of the Eylesbarrow tin mine

Down Tor (581694), from where there are impressive views of Burrator Reservoir.

From the tor head south of east, soon reaching, and following, a wall on the right, then heading due east to reach the western end of a fine stone row (587693).

D Down Tor Stone Row

Technically the row is on Hingston Hill, but is invariably referred to as the Down Tor row. It is impressive, one of Dartmoor's best, being almost 400 yards (about 350m) long and with a menhir about 10ft (3m) high at its western end. This tall menhir forms part of a cairn circle, a stone circle surrounding a burial mound. The row is also aligned with a large cairn (about 52ft/16m in diameter) about 250 yards (229m) to the east. Close to that cairn is a small enclosure. There are hut circles on Down Tor's southern flank and also to the north-east, but can this remote enclosure really have been an animal pound?

Down Tor prehistoric cairn circle and stone row

e Having viewed the stone row, head south towards Combshead Tor, but, unless wishing to go to the top of this tor or to visit Cuckoo Rock (584687), bear left to go around its marshy eastern flank (to about 590688), avoiding the stream on your right which runs into tin-mining ruins. Now contour around the hill to the left, then go south, downhill, at any convenient point to reach a clear track west-south-west downhill. Just before reaching the Scout Hut (about 150 yards (130m) before it) a leat crosses the track. A worthwhile detour – adding about 1 mile (1.6km) to the walk – turns right along this leat to reach two 1917 boundary markers. Here, cross the leat and head north-west to reach a curious series of stone circles.

E Yellowmead Down stone Circles

There are four concentric circles here with diameters of 20, 38, 48 and 65ft (6, 11.5, 14.5 and 20m). The stones of the inner circle are so close they almost form a continuous ring of stones. If stone circles are enigmatic this site is quadruply so.

f If the detour has been followed, reverse the outward route in e, returning to the main track and turn right. Go past the Scout Hut, to the left, and continue to the start.

WESTERN BEACON AND THE ERME VALLEY

MAPS:
Most of the route on Harvey Dartmoor South, OS Landranger Sheet 202, OS Outdoor Leisure Sheet 28

START/FINISH:
Ivybridge. The 'official' start point of the Two Moors Way is the Bridge Inn at the centre of the town; there are large car parks here (636561)

Stagecoach Devon bus 39, which links Plymouth and Exeter, and Western National bus X80, which links Torquay and Plymouth, both stop at the Ivybridge Town Hall. Ivybridge also has a railway station on the eastern edge of the town

DISTANCE/ASCENT:
8 miles (13km)/1,100ft (335m)

APPROXIMATE TIME:
5 hours

HIGHEST POINT:
Butterdon Hill 1,204ft (367m)

REFRESHMENTS:
There is something for everyone in Ivybridge

ADVICE:
A very straightforward route, with an easy to follow moorland section and a valley section on good paths. Some sections can be muddy after rain. Watch out for tree roots across paths

Starting from Ivybridge, on the southern edge of the National Park, this route follows the Two Moors Way, then visits the fine viewpoint of Western Beacon before following a moorland ridge northwards. The return is through a picturesque hamlet and along the wooded valley of the River Erme.

Hangershell Rock

Harford Church

A Ivybridge

Ivybridge is a relatively modern town – though the bridge of the name, which crossed the Erme, was mentioned in a 13th century charter – growing up around a successful paper mill, at Stowford, as lately as the 19th century. It is famous among railway enthusiasts for its viaduct. The original viaduct, built by Isambard Kingdom Brunel in wood, did not stand up well to the rigours of the GWR trains and was replaced in 1893 by an eight-arched granite and brick structure towering above the River Erme.

a From the Bridge Inn (636563) go north along Harford Road, with the River Erme to your left for the first few steps. The road steepens and bears right; continue along it, passing a school on the right. Go straight over at a cross-roads to reach a sign for the National Park and a stone commemorating the opening of the Two Moors Way.

B Two Moors Way

This long-distance route is an 'unofficial' trail, that is not one specified and maintained by Act of Parliament and the Countryside Commission. The route is waymarked and maintained by Devon County Council. It was opened in 1976 having been surveyed by the Devon Ramblers Association. It is 102 miles (163km) long and links Ivybridge, at the southern edge of the Dartmoor National Park, with Lynton on the Bristol Channel Coast. The path traverses both the Dartmoor and Exmoor National Parks. On Dartmoor it avoids the high northern moorland, taking a route around its eastern edge. Some would see this is as a soft option, but in taking this line the route avoids the problems which the Dartmoor ranges might cause for a walker attempting to complete the route in

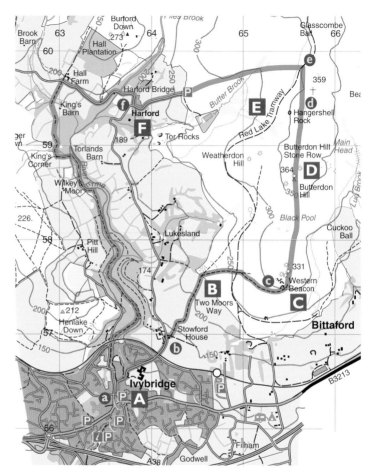

one multi-day outing, and allows walkers with limited experience of the wild moor to complete a worthwhile route across fine country.

b　Cross Stowford Bridge over the railway line, and continue for 300 yards (274m) to reach Stowford House on the left. There, turn right along a signed bridleway, but almost immediately go left along another track, following it to reach a gate on to open moorland. Here we leave the Two Moors Way, which heads north-west towards the shallow pass between Butterdon and Weatherdon Hills. Our route goes right, just north of east, on a path that is sometimes distinct, at other times less so, but always aiming for the tors of Western Beacon.

C Western Beacon

The beacon is the southernmost peak of Dartmoor and lies at the end of a long finger of high moorland, allowing wide views in all directions except northwards. To the south is Ivybridge with the South Devon coast beyond. To the west is the Erme Valley, the trees giving the line of our return route. Eastwards is the fine country around Ugborough and South Brent.

The peak is grass moor, a complete contrast to the bog moors further north. Look out for the whinchat, a characteristic bird of this type of moorland, and for characteristic flowers such as tormentil and heath bedstraw.

c Head north, crossing Western Beacon's broad summit (654575), then descending to the shallow Black Pool which lies at the equally shallow col between the Beacon and

Please note: time taken calculated according to the Naismith Formula (see p.2)

The memorial to John Prideaux in Harford Church

Butterdon Hill. As there are so few pools on Dartmoor the walker will usually see ponies drinking here. A well-defined path follows a series of boundary stones to the top of Butterdon Hill (655586), another fine viewpoint; there is also a lovely little tor. From it, continue along the path and the boundary stones, with Hangershell Rock (seen to better effect from later in the walk) to the left. You are also following the line of a very long stone row.

D   Butterdon Hill Stone Row

The row (of single stones) starts at a barrow/retaining circle near the summit of the hill and once extended for over 1 mile (1.6km) north towards Piles Hill. Unfortunately much of the northern end of the row was destroyed in the 19th century, possibly because the stones were used to form the row of boundary markers. Ironically the boundary roughly follows the line of the old row.

d   Just beyond Hangershell Rock and the stone row the path reaches (at 655599) the line of the old Red Lake Tramway (which has been followed by the Two Moors Way) and an east-west bridleway.

E   Red Lake Tramway

The tramway was built in 1912 to carry equipment and workers to the china clay pits at Red Lake, to the north-west of the Avon Reservoir. The china clay was not brought down on the tramway, being pumped as a liquid down a long pipeline (see Note to Walk 20).

e   When you reach the tramway, turn left (W) downhill choosing your own route on good ground. There is no path, but the way (a bridleway) is obvious enough using a natural hollow, and crossing the stream which feeds the small reservoir lower down on your left, to reach a road end at Harford Moor Gate (at 644595). Go through the gate and follow the road down into Harford.

F   Harford

Harford is a lovely hamlet with a beautiful church dedicated to St. Petroc. Inside, there is a marvellous barrel roof supported by granite columns. Also worth noting is the table tomb with a brass effigy in 16th century armour. This is thought to be the tomb of Thomas Williams of Stowford who was Speaker of Parliament at the time of Elizabeth I. John Prideaux, another local man, also has a memorial showing him kneeling with his family. Prideaux was a Bishop of Worcester.

f In the hamlet bear right and north, past the church, following the lane around a sharp left-hand bend and steeply downhill to Harford Bridge over the Erme. Continue along the lane for another ½ mile (800m) to reach a lane for Hall Farm (630597), on the right. Here, turn left (SSW) along a track. At its end, with the fine King's Barn (630597) off to the left, take the path heading east of south, crossing a field to reach a signpost which points the way through a copse of sweet chestnut trees. Now follow a path through bracken to another signpost by a gate (near King's Corner 630589). Go through and turn left, as indicated, following the path down to a small stream. Cross this and continue, soon reaching the River Erme.

Turn right and follow the Erme's right (western) bank through magnificent wooded country where it can be muddy after rain. The path is mostly close to the river, offering a delightful noisy dimension to the woodland. Go under the railway and continue between the river, left, and a road, right, to reach the bridge in the centre of Ivybridge. The Bridge Inn is now just a step away.

The railway viaduct over the River Erme at Ivybridge

BRENT MOOR AND THE AVON

MAPS:
Harvey Dartmoor South, OS
Landranger Sheet 202, OS
Outdoor Leisure Sheet 28

START/FINISH:
At 681629, the car park at
Shipley Bridge, reached by a
minor road following the River
Avon north from South Brent

No buses serve Shipley Bridge.
The closest stop is at South
Brent, about 3 miles (5km) to
the south. South Brent is on
the line of the Stagecoach
Devon and Western National
buses which follow the A38

DISTANCE/ASCENT:
9½ miles (15.3km)/1,100ft
(335m)

APPROXIMATE TIME:
3½ hours

HIGHEST POINT:
Petre's Cross 1,578ft (481m)

REFRESHMENTS:
None on the route, though
there is often an ice cream van
at the car park in summer;
South Brent south of route

ADVICE:
A quite long, and therefore
demanding, walk, but with
some good tracks and features
to aid the walker. A compass is
useful in poor visibility,
particularly over Brent Moor
where good landmarks are
lacking other than the Bala
Brook

Ryder's Hill is the highest peak on the southern moor, dominating an area of wild beauty. This walk explores the wilderness south of the hill, around the Avon Reservoir.

a   From the southern end of the car park (681629), just to the west of Shipley Bridge, take the rising stony track, heading towards a wall which you need to keep to your left as you continue north-west, crossing the tarmac waterworks road (678630). The steep path to the same point, starting a little north of the first, offers the interest of passing the ruins of the former naphtha works.

A   Hunter's Stone
The stone is a memorial to four friends and fox hunters whose names were carved on it by a fellow hunter. The four names appear on the sides and the top, together with a fifth, presumably the name of the carver. Names are Treby, Bulteel, Trelawny (sides) and Carew or Carey, and Coryton (top).

b   The track, which follows the path of the old Zeal Tramway, ascends alongside the wall until the wall ends (675631), maintaining direction, roughly parallel to the valley of the Bala Brook (to the left). The track soon veers north-west, then north, as the valley bends to the right.

Hunter's Stone

B Zeal Tramway

The tramway was built in 1847 when an attempt was made to create a naphtha industry based on peat extraction from Red Lake Mire. Naphtha is an aromatic hydrocarbon extracted from any fossil fuel. It was used as the basic ingredient for mothballs. The tramway had granite sleepers and wooden rails, horses being used to haul trucks to the naphtha extraction plant at Shipley Bridge. After three years the venture failed, but a few years later the tramway was bought and restored by a company extracting china clay from Petre's Pit (at 659648, and passed by our walk) and from another kaolin mine close to Red Lake.

c   While the tramway is clear at first as it climbs steadily up Zeal Hill on to Brent Moor, it gradually becomes less obvious and other ways appear, heading in the same direction. Care is required with navigation as this is a stretch of moor which can be difficult in poor weather. Watch for the way to bend again, to the left (NW), getting nearer to the Bala Brook, still on your left, and closing in where the stream valley bears left by the intersection of the Jobber's Path (666646). Soon the tramway reappears and is more easily followed as it crosses the high flat moor north of Quickbeam Hill, keeping a little above Petre's Pit (659648), near which the Bala Brook rises. The hump of Eastern White Barrow (665652) in the near distance, east-north-east of Petre's Pit may be a useful landmark. We now make for Petre's Cross (654655) by Western White Barrow.

A sycamore tree presides over the ruins of Huntingdon Warren

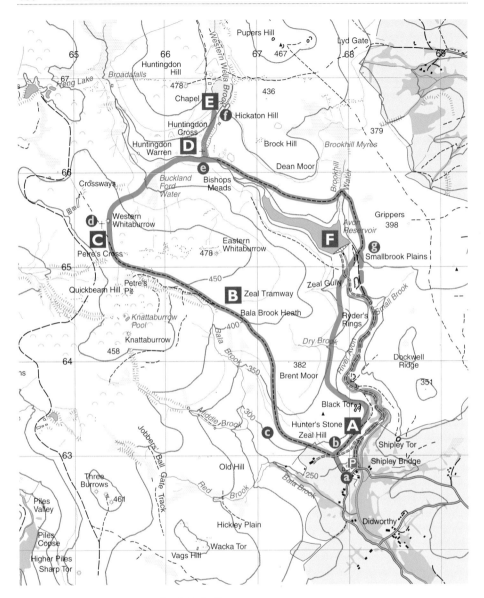

C   Petre's Cross

The name remembers a cross erected as a boundary marker by Sir William Petre in the late 16th century. The cross was mounted on Western White Barrow, a large Bronze Age cairn. After the Dissolution of the Monasteries Petre bought some of the estates land of Buckfast Abbey and marked his boundary with that of the Royal Forest of Dartmoor by erecting a number of boundary crosses. Sir William died in 1571. After the building of the tramway in 1847 workers on the line used the stones of the cairn to build themselves a hut against Dartmoor's cruel winters. They used Petre's Cross as a door lintel, knocking off the arms to make it a better fit. The ruins of the hut still offer protection against the wind, if not the rain. The cross shaft has now been re-erected on the cairn, though it is not easy to see which stone it is: it is about 4ft (1.2m) long, but embedded in the cairn. Apparently it is upside down.

d From Petre's Cross the entrenched tramway continues north-north-west towards Red Lake with its cone of china clay debris. Our route now follows the remotest section of the Two Moors Way (see Note to Walk 25): head north, going downhill towards an old spoil heap (650658) to reach a crossing track (at 650659). Turn right (E), following the track (OS (another) Abbot's Way) to the River Avon. If the river is high, the easiest crossing place is a clapper bridge at 657662. However, as this bridge lies to the west of the Abbot's Way's route along the Avon Valley, the decision to use it is best made at a point where the

Huntingdon Cross on the left bank of the River Avon

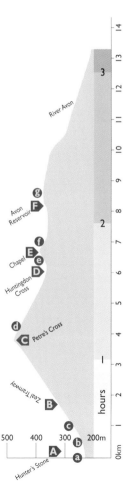

The Avon Reservoir on southern Dartmoor

Avon Valley is clearly visible (657659). Having crossed the Avon, continue west along the left (northern) bank to reach the next landmark, Huntingdon Cross (664662).

D Huntingdon Cross

The cross, at 5ft (1.5m) high and with its arms intact, is much better preserved than Petre's Cross, though it dates from the same year, being another boundary marker of Sir William Petre's acquired monastic estates. It takes its name from the hill to the north, now marked on maps as Huntingdon Warren because of its extensive rabbit warren. There are pillow mounds (see Note to Walk 5) to the north-west of the cross on the hillside. There are also Bronze Age hut circles further up the hill.

e   From the cross a very worthwhile detour heads north along the valley of the Western Wella Brook, staying on the left (eastern) bank. You soon pass the ruins of a waterwheel house erected by tin miners, then reach the sad ruins of a chapel.

E   Chapel

The chapel was built by the Martin brothers and others who wanted the miners, warreners and other remote moorland workers to have a place of worship. One of the brothers was the Rev. W. Keble Martin, the famous compiler/illustrator of *The Concise British Flora*.

f   Return to Huntingdon Cross and head east along a rough track that soon veers east-south-east along the hillside above the Avon reservoir, to the right. The track passes close to Bronze Age hut circles then reaches Brockhill Stream (679658). Cross this and turn right to follow it. Soon, bear left away from the stream to reach the end of the reservoir's dam.

F   Avon Reservoir

The dam behind which the reservoir formed was built in 1954, after the creation of the National Park, with an understandable debate about the correctness of such an undertaking, however, the views are wonderful.

g   The direct route can be followed from the east side of the dam (681653), taking the wider track, which forks slightly left here, passing an enclosed area to your right (Bronze Age settlement 681648) and quickly joining the tarmac road following the Avon (Long-a-Traw) between the dam and the car park, which stays by the river and passes the Hunter's Stone.

A more scenic route involves a short climb and follows the rim of the western escarpment. Opposite the dam take the steeper right fork down to the road below. Cross the reservoir road to the west and almost opposite there is a small path which climbs the escarpment to the west of the valley, leading diagonally to a point where the escarpment above Long-a-Traw disappears round the corner. Follow this path upwards to the corner where the ground flattens and the remains of a wall lie ahead. Here you will find the Bronze Age settlement of Ryder's Rings (OS Rider's Rings, 680645). From the southern end of the Rings follow a small path heading south and, keeping below the rim of the escarpment on its right, head for Black Tor (681635). From here either contour south-west on a trackless but easy grass moor, leading you to the waterworks entrance above the car park, or south into a belt of conifers, joining a track which bears to the right (SW) at the southern end of the copse, and is then followed until it divides several ways. Both routes meet by the wall along the waterworks boundary. Cross the tarmac road and descend to the car park, reversing your outward route.

THE ERME PLAINS AND STALL MOOR

MAPS:
Harvey Dartmoor South,
OS Landranger Sheet 202,
Outdoor Leisure Sheet 28

START/FINISH:
At 625611, the end of the track to the Water Treatment Works. Follow the road that runs north-east of Torr, a small hamlet to the north-east of Cornwood, taking the left fork. Go through the gate on the moor (New Waste) where there is parking on the left and right. Do not obstruct the lane on the left

No buses serve the start point. The closest are DevonBuses 58 and 59 which stop at Cornwood, about 3 miles (5km) south-west of the start

DISTANCE/ASCENT:
9 miles (14.5km)/900ft (275m)

APPROXIMATE TIME:
5½ hours

HIGHEST POINT:
Langcombe Hill 1,555ft (474m)

REFRESHMENTS:
Cornwood and Ivybridge

ADVICE:
Straightforward in its early stages, but needing navigation skills for Yealm Head to Langcombe Hill and Erme Head which is a featureless moorland section of the route

To the north of Ivybridge lies the longest prehistoric stone row in Europe. This walk traverses one of Dartmoor's finest wildernesses and follows part of the row.

A   Dendles Wood and Hawns

Eric Hemery has described the glen containing these ancient, semi-natural woodlands, covered in moss and lichen, and littered with huge boulders, as well as many concealed archaeological features, as a unique but lost fairyland. It is therefore fitting that the Dartmoor National Park Authority, with the aid of Heritage Lottery Funds, were able to acquire it in 1997 for regeneration. Already an intrusive plantation of conifers has been cut down, and work on an unprecedented scale in this country, is proceeding to recreate some of the

The stone circle at the southern end of the Erme stone row

Erme Pound seen from the walk
on the opposite bank of the
River Erme

moorland and to rehabilitate the woodlands. Ultimately the aim is to provide low-key recreational, interpretative and educational use of the site.

a Follow the clear track left (N) from the moor gate, following a stream alongside and soon reaching another gate (625616). Our way continues north, passing Dendles Wood on the left, and a hut group (623625). Continue across Ranny Brook (near the top end of the woodlands) and contour round to Yealm Steps (618637), passing a series of small waterfalls. The river, now a stream, leads you up to its source at Yealm Head (1,387ft/423m) (615649), Stall Moor being to the right (E). The route onwards is north-north-east (22°), untracked but manageable, to Langcombe Hill: first passing the OS trig point (1,554ft/474m) to your left, and keeping to the east of marshy ground. From the final flattish top (1,540ft/469m; at 620663) with its tumulus and boundary stone, continue over open moor north-north-east, to Erme Head (621669).

B Erme Pits

This collection of debris piles and depressions, the remnants of a Medieval tin mine, was recorded as Armed Pit in a 1672 survey. The use of Arme instead of Erme, though probably little more than a dialect difference, was still a popular pronunciation until the mid-20th century.

b Follow the right-hand (S) bank of the Erme, east-south-east, passing Erme Pits, and rounding the corner between Stinger's Hill and Brown Heath, to continue southwards. The path passes through 'the Meadow', still beside the river in a small gorge.

C Erme Stone Row and Erme Pound

Erme Pound is an assembly of prehistoric walls and hut circles (see Note to Walk 7). The stone row is 2.1 miles (3.4km) long, longer than any of the famed Carnac alignments (though, of course, they consist of many parallel rows). In fact, the Erme row is the longest prehistoric stone row in Europe and,

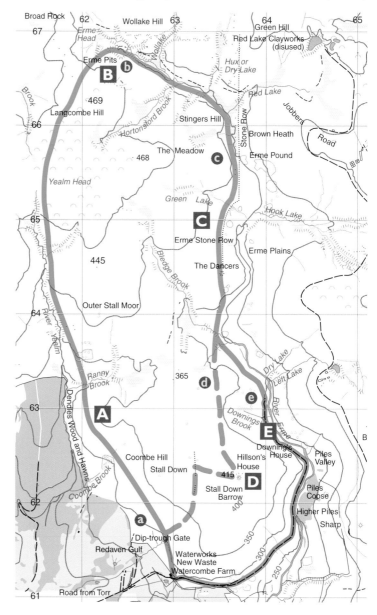

probably, in the world. It is even more intriguing for not being straight, for although it heads almost due north from the start here on the Erme Plains to its end on Green Hill, it swings right, left and right again as it crosses the undulating moor around the River Erme's Valley. It also crosses the river and Red Lake. The line of sight along the row is not continuous and it seems that the row was reasonably aligned only when sections were visible, suggesting that it could have been constructed piecemeal by teams working on different sections. At the Green Hill end (on the hill's summit, though it's not a conspicuous top) there is a burial cairn. There is also a cairn at the southern end of the stone row, enclosed by a stone circle about 55ft (17m) in diameter and consisting of about 25 stones. The circle is occasionally called The Dancers (or Cornwood Maidens), an old legend maintaining that a group of young people were turned to stone for the sin of dancing on a Sunday. This legend recalls the similar story naming The Hurlers on Bodmin Moor over the Cornish border and that at Nine Maidens (see note to Walk 8).

The stones of the row decrease in height from the circle as the row heads north, though the scope for this rapidly ends. What is also notable is that the row seems complete – though there are gaps on Green Hill – the tinners having left the stones alone when searching for material for their own buildings. As there are tin ruins all along the Erme close to the row this is remarkable, particularly as it is known that at other moorland sites the megalithic sites were used as convenient quarries. It seems that the tinners had much more respect for the 'old men' of the moor than did later moor dwellers. Indeed, it is claimed that if they needed to disturb a site for their own workings – leat digging etc. – they would restore it afterwards. The true purpose of the stone row remains an enigma, though it has been suggested that it defined a processional way between The Dancers stone circle and the burial chamber on Green Hill.

c   The Erme Stone Row crosses the Erme (637656) and we follow its impressive line southwards away from the riverside. Across the river, left, you will see Erme Pound (638656) and Hook Lake; on your left too is the superb valley bog of Erme Plains (see Note to Walk 22). At the southern end of the stone row the stone circle (635644), sometimes known as The Dancers; we then take a convenient path south to Bledge Brook (OS also called Blatchford Bottom) where it meets the Erme (635637).

D   Stall Down and Hillson's House

As with the Erme row, the stone row on Stall Down (OS

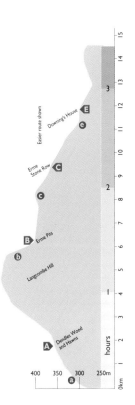

Please note: time taken calculated according to the Naismith Formula (see p.2)

Erme Pits – an ancient tinwork

Stalldown) is aligned almost due north, and, again similar to Erme, it is not perfectly straight, executing a shallow left curve as it heads north. It also has graded stones but here the taller stones are at the northern end, the tallest of them almost 9ft (nearly 3m) high. In that sense, though shorter than Erme, the Stall Down row is more impressive.

There are several cairns near the row, though, interestingly, they lie to its side not at the ends. There are also other cairns to the east on the actual summit of the Down. The stones of one of these were used to build a small, now ruinous, hut called Hillson's House. It seems an unlikely place for a tinners' hut, though it might have been used by a shepherd. However, local legend maintains that a local man found a child abandoned on Stall Moor and that he and his wife raised it as their own, calling the boy Hillson from his origin. When he was old enough the boy returned to the moor, building the little hut on Stall Down and living there, supporting himself by building eight-day clocks, several of which are said to survive in the neighbourhood. It is an intriguing story and clearly based on some element of truth. The name Hillson is not common, but is a local one, so perhaps a local boy really did turn his back on family life for the wilderness.

d   From Bledge Brook you can steer a course for the ridge, south-south-east, then south, over Stall Down Barrow (OS Stalldown Barrow), following the stone row (at 632624) southwards and, from its southern end, turning south-west to the gate (625616) we passed through at the beginning of the walk. From here follow the track south to the start.

E   Downing's House
The house is a tinners' cache, and a much better documented one than the Beehive Hut passed on Walk 7. The hiding places were for tools when the tinners left the moor and, occasionally, for illicit alcohol stills – or so it is said. The House was also once known as Smugglers' Hole because of a persistent story that it was used to store contraband landed on the South Devon coast. Downing's House is much more substantial than the usual hiding places, having a roof and being roomy enough for someone to spend an emergency night in reasonable comfort.

e   After crossing Bledge Brook, the easier option, however, is to continue by the Erme to a weir (640632), first passing the remains of a tinner's hut and a blowing house. The way onwards, along the old tramway, is easy, shortly passing Downing's House (639629), and on the other side of the river, Piles Wood, one of at least three oak copses on Dartmoor (see Note to Walk 5). Next pass through Bronze Age settlements (638613), with hut circles on both sides, the track finally reaching the modern waterworks (630612). Bear to the right here and make for the northern end of the wall east of the works. Follow the wall north-west, then west to the gate we passed on the outward route (625616), and go south to the car park at New Waste.

Crossing Langcombe Hill

28 DARTMOUTH

MAPS:
OS Landranger Sheet 202,
Outdoor Leisure Sheet 20

START/FINISH:
Dartmouth. In summer parking can be a problem, though there are several car parks

Dartmouth is served by Western National bus 93 which links the town with Plymouth. This bus stops at Stoke Fleming for walkers wishing to complete a linear walk from Dartmouth to Stoke Fleming. Kingswear, across the river, has a railway station and a ferry link to Dartmouth. The X89 links Totnes and Dartmouth, while the 22 From Brixham and the 200 from Paignton both stop in Kingswear

DISTANCE/ASCENT:
5½ miles (9km)/650ft (200m). The walk to Stoke Fleming is 4 miles (6km)

APPROXIMATE TIME:
2½–3 hours

HIGHEST POINT:
530ft (160m) on Jawbone Lane

REFRESHMENTS:
None on the walk, but there are plenty available at Dartmouth; also at Stoke Fleming

ADVICE:
Fairly easy and straightforward walking

Our first walk in South Devon starts from one of England's most picturesque and historic ports, set on the side of the river which both named the moor on which it rises, and has formed the backdrop to some of our moorland walks. From Dartmouth, the walk follows a section of the South West Coast Path, Britain's longest National Trail.

The harbour, Dartmouth

A Dartmouth

Though the Dart's estuary is wide and sheltered, its banks are steep and in ancient times plastered with the mud that accumulates on all tidal rivers – an unlikely spot for a major port. There was a Saxon settlement, but the Saxons lived at the top of the western valley side, calling their village Dunestal, the hamlet on the hill, a name which forms the basis of Townstal, the upper section of today's town. Later, the Saxons expanded, creating two small fishing ports on the river, these ports eventually linking with each other, across reclaimed land, and with the hill settlement to form Dartmouth.

The new port expanded quickly and by the 12th century was large enough, and important enough, to be the starting point for the Second and Third Crusades. The grant of borough status by Edward III in 1341 improved the prosperity of the port to such an extent that when, in 1346, the king called for ships to enforce a siege of Calais, only two English ports bettered Dartmouth's fleet of 31. Dartmouth's contribution did not go unnoticed by the French who, in revenge, made several raids on the port, causing the first fortifications to be raised at the river's mouth. The overseer of this work, in part, was the town mayor John Hawley who is thought to have been Chaucer's model for the Shipman in the prologue to *The Canterbury Tales*.

The Buttery, Dartmouth

As a port, Dartmouth's prosperity was based not only on fishing, but on trade with France – once peace was established – the countries of the Mediterranean and with the New World. In 1620 the Pilgrim Fathers berthed at Dartmouth on their way to America, the *Speedwell* requiring urgent repairs. Despite the repairs *Speedwell* only reached Plymouth from where the entire expedition continued in their second ship, *Mayflower*.

As ships became larger, the limitations of Dartmouth's position became apparent and trade moved elsewhere. But the town remained important to the Royal Navy. In 1863 a college was set up in *Britannia* and *Hindustan*, two old wooden warships, to train officers. At the turn of the century the old ships were replaced by a new, purpose-built, college built to the north, above the town. Designed by Sir Aston Webb, who was also the architect for the Victoria and Albert Museum and Admiralty Arch, the college, which took the name Britannia, still dominates the northern end of Dartmouth.

The town is well worth a leisurely exploration. Its most picturesque spot is the early 17th century Butterwalk, its first floor supported by the columns of the walk, its upper storeys overhung and gable-topped. The Butterwalk was built on reclaimed land and originally backed on to the river. In the Butterwalk, Dartmouth's museum explores the history of the town. Its curious uneven stairway was apparently deliberate, created to cause unfamiliar (and unwanted) night visitors to trip and so wake the dogs.

Also worth visiting is the Newcomen Engine House (and Tourist Information Office). Thomas Newcomen was a Dartmouth man, an ironmonger by trade and inventor by hobby. In 1712 he built a steam engine which was used to pump water from Cornish and Devon mines. The Engine House stands at the edge of Royal Avenue Gardens, extremely attractive gardens laid out in Victorian times (when the bandstand was completed) but redesigned in 1991.

In the centre of Dartmouth is a picturesque harbour, which gives some idea of the extent of the river before land reclamation. On its river side is the old Dartmouth station, which is now the Station Restaurant. Dartmouth was unique in having a railway station, but no railway. When the railway came to the area Dartmouth was too steep for a line, but set up its own station with ticket sales and staff. Passengers were ferried across the river to the line at Kingswear.

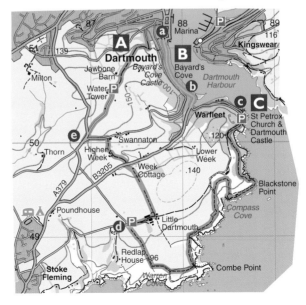

a From the station, follow the river southwards. At the end of South Embankment, bear right into Cole's Court, then left to reach the Lower Ferry, the earliest ferry across the river. By 1834 the rowing boat had been replaced by a larger, but still rowed, craft which could take two horses and carts. Dartmouth also has a Higher Ferry (at the northern end of the town). Go past the ferry slipway, passing Agincourt House, a merchant's house, on the right, to reach Bayard's Cove.

B Bayard's Cove

It was from here that the early Crusades departed, as did Walter Raleigh on several trips to America. Later, the Pilgrim Fathers left from here and the East India Company used the cove for their early trips.

At the southern end of the cove is Bearcove Castle (Bearcove being the local pronunciation of Bayard's Cove), built by Henry VIII as a second line of defence – after Dartmouth Castle to the south. The castle had eleven cannons aimed across the river, though their range of fire was so limited they were unlikely to have been very effective.

b Climb either of the two sets of steps into Newcomen Road and turn left, following the road (which changes name twice) to reach Castle Road on the left. Take this, following it past One Gun Point, a self-explanatory headland, to reach St Petrox Church. Continue to follow the signs for Dartmouth Castle (886502).

C St Petrox Church and Dartmouth Castle

Petrox was a 6th century Celtic saint who is thought to have had a hermit cell near the site of the present church. There was probably a Saxon church here and perhaps an early Norman one, but there is no record of a church until 1192. That building may well have been connected with a curious incident of sacred body snatching. Petrox's remains were entombed at Bodmin Priory, but monks from St Meen, near Rennes in Brittany, where the saint was held in high esteem, mounted a raid, stealing the relics. The outraged Prior Roger of Bodmin appealed to Henry II for the return of the remains and the king ordered their confiscation. They were transported to Winchester, then by sea to the West Country and from there to Bodmin where the chest that once held them can still be seen. The exact sea route is not known, but it is conjectured that the remains landed at Dartmouth and that the church was built in commemoration. The church had a light which burned each night as a landmark for sailors, but

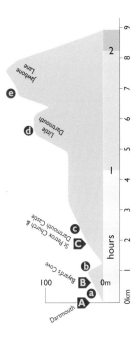

Please note: time taken calculated according to the Naismith Formula (see p.2)

had fallen into disrepair by the time of the Civil War when it was used as a grain store. It was then rebuilt; inside there are several fine monuments, including a large brass to John Roope who died in 1609.

The ruined tower and part of the old wall of Dartmouth Castle form part of the original structure from John Hawley's time. At that time the castle was augmented by a chain stretched across the river. In 1462 the king granted £30 to improve the defences, though construction of the castle we now see did not start until 1481. Dartmouth is interesting in being the first castle in Britain to have been built primarily for artillery, with gun ports constructed to maximise the range of fire. The armament was flat-bed mounted cannons, wheeled trolleys not being introduced until Henry VIII's time. The cannons that now greet visitors are the original, flat-bed guns, now trolley-mounted.

The castle was modified over the centuries, an additional protective earthwork being added on Gallant's Bower during the Civil War when the area was held by the Royalists. Gallant's Bower was destroyed by Parliament, but the castle was maintained, then enlarged in 1672 when a Dutch invasion was feared. It was strengthened again in 1861 when a French invasion seemed possible following the outbreak of the American War of Independence, and garrisoned in 1940 against a possible German invasion.

c   Ignore the signs for Castle Cove, and opposite the castle ticket office take the signed path, heading south and zig-zagging upwards. The South West Coast Path – watch carefully for signs which are sometimes well hidden – then meets a road below Gallants Bower, but quickly bears off left, going down steeply to the south-east (885501). The path hugs

Looking towards Stoke Fleming village from Warren Point

the coast, crossing a wave-cut platform and rounding Blackstone Point (where there was a gun battery in the 17th century) to reach a point above Compass Cove, where the ways divide. Here we need to avoid going down the path to the sea (signed Compass Cove) or going up the road to Compass Cove and the Coastguard Station. The old cottages here, were once the home of Revenue men chasing smugglers using the estuary and local coves. The way straight ahead takes you down to Compass Cove, so bear to the right, to follow the Coast Path (waymarked, on the *far* side of the stile).

The path beyond the stile leads into a shallow valley (still sticking to the signed coastal path), from which you climb back steeply to the cliff top, following it closely until you reach Combe Point (881487). Continue west along the Coast Path, and after about 1 mile (1.6km) you reach a kissing gate where the path turns inland, cutting off a section of cliffs above Warren Cove. Follow the path alongside a couple of fields, through another kissing gate and into the NT parking area (874492).

Dartmouth Castle

d Here the short version of the walk, requiring a bus return to Dartmouth, goes left, following the National Trail along the minor road into the lovely village of Stoke Fleming.

The full route turns right (ENE) opposite the car park, following a track to Little Dartmouth. Here ignore the right-hand lane to the big house and continue up to the cottages where a sharp left-hand turn is signposted 'Week Cottage ½ mile'. This lane opens onto two fields where you walk parallel (NNW) to the right-hand fence, passing the cottage to your right to a gate on to a drive leading to the B3205. Turn left and then right along a path leading to Higher Week. At Swannerton Farm the path is waymarked between the buildings and you then cross in front of the bungalow to a drive which skirts its left-hand side and then leads to the minor road. Turn left and follow the road to its junction with the main road (the A379).

e Turn right, with great care, for a few yards, then go right again (at 870501) along Jawbone Lane (not named, but vehicles are prohibited 500 yards (457m) ahead). Follow the lane north-east gently downhill to Jawbone Barn, then much more steeply down as the hill descends towards Dartmouth. The lane offers a tremendous view of Dartmouth and the Britannia Naval College as it descends. The lane ends at a T-junction with Crowther's Hill: turn right and follow the hill down into the centre of the town.

SLAPTON LEY

To the south of Dartmouth, near the village of Slapton a sand bar separates the sea from a freshwater lake which is a haven for wildlife. This walk visits the lake and sand bar.

Looking north along Slapton Sands from near Torcross

MAPS:
OS Landranger Sheet 202,
Outdoor Leisure Sheet 20

START/FINISH:
At 829444 the car park at the edge of Slapton Sands, near the turning to Slapton village. Parking is also available at the southern end of the Ley, near Torcross

Western National bus 93 which links Dartmouth with Plymouth stops at Slapton village, Slapton turn, Torcross and Stokenham

DISTANCE/ASCENT:
6½ miles (10.5 km)/550ft (170m); 8 miles (13km) including Slapton Village

HIGHEST POINT:
Coleridge Cross 354ft (108m)

REFRESHMENTS:
Numerous – at Torcross, Stokenham and Slapton

ADVICE:
Straightforward, though the walk along Slapton Sands can be tiring

A   D-Day Monument

The tall obelisk to the north of the start point was erected by the US Government and unveiled in 1954 by General Grunthur of the US Army to commemorate the use of the immediate area as a practice ground for the Normandy landings due to similarities between Slapton Sands and Omaha beach. On 13 November 1943 the folk of seven local villages were given until 20 December to vacate their homes and the area because the rehearsals were to involve the use of live ammunition. Despite the short days, the appalling weather and the fact that most of the young men were away fighting, the evacuation was completed on time, and the area became a military range. Part of Slapton, and other villages, were destroyed and rats the size of dogs were seen scampering through the deserted streets and eating the putty from the window frames of the deserted houses (or so it is said). On a lighter note, if such can exist in so grim a tale, one old lady is said to have ignored the prohibition order and driven back to her house, only to be met by a column of army vehicles in a narrow road. Awe-struck and unable either to pass or turn around, the old lady sat tight as a mobile army crane lifted her (and her car) into a nearby field. The column moved on.

a   From the car park either follow the path south-south-west between the main road (crossing it with care) and Slapton Ley – this is the route of the South West Coast Path – or follow the shingle bar to Torcross.

B   Slapton Sands and Bee Sands

The name is a misnomer, the bar being shingle rather than sand. It was created by changes in beach level following the last Ice Age, the raised bank trapping the outflow of several small streams and creating the Ley. The Ley was of enormous value to the inhabitants of Slapton village in medieval times, providing them with a 'moat', a protection against pirates and other sea-borne raiders. The downside was, of course, that the Ley also impeded their access to the sea. The solution was a drawbridge at the narrow point of the Ley, where the road from the sands now crosses the bridge to reach the village.

b   Climb the steps beyond the Torcross Hotel, still following the South West Coast Path, but also from here a signed circular walk. Continue along the path as it circles Beesands Quarry (disused), but just beyond the quarry turn right off the coast path, at the top of the steps (821414).

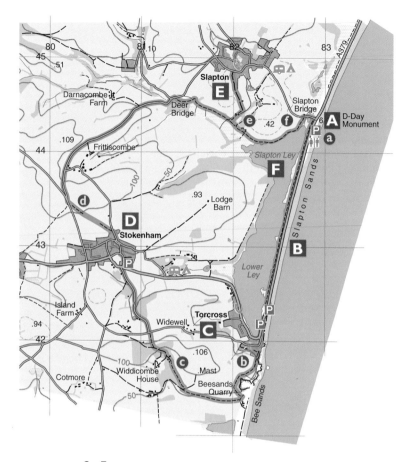

C Torcross

Torcross is now defended from the sea not only by the shingle bar, but by a sea wall erected after a violent storm in the winter of 1978/79 severely damaged the little village. Close to the village – at the southern end of the car park on the Ley side – is a Sherman tank retrieved from the sea in 1984. During the rehearsals off Slapton, the US army practised landing craft assaults while surface ships shelled the area over the heads of the seaborne troops. During one practice, using live rounds to 'toughen' the troops, Slapton beach was shelled after the troops had disembarked, around 50 soldiers being killed. Disastrous though this was, it was completely dwarfed by a later tragedy when, just six weeks before D-Day, during a full-scale rehearsal, the landing craft convoy was surprised by German E-boats. The Royal Navy's convoy escort had been reduced to one slow support vessel because of an earlier accident to a destroyer, and due to farcical mix-ups the escort was not told of the approach of the E-boats and was using a different radio frequency to the American convoy. The loss of 3 LSTs (landing craft designed to carry tanks) almost caused the cancellation of the 6 June landings.

News of the disaster was suppressed, not only because of its potential affect on morale, but because the news would have revealed the existence of the secret rehearsals and, therefore, the real landings. After the war ended the disaster was still kept secret and only within the last decade or so has the full truth become known. Almost 800 men died in the engagement: the tank at Torcross is a silent memorial to them.

c Continue along the path heading inland (W) and following the signs for Widewell, going over three stiles and into a pleasant wood. Follow the path through the wood – to the left, beyond the wood, is Widdicombe House, dating from the 18th century, but on the site of a much earlier building. Avoid turnings to the left. Continue along the path, passing two cottages to the left, to reach a three-way path junction (811419). Here bear right and follow the track north to reach a minor road at a T-junction (811421).

Cross over to the road opposite, and maintain direction going downhill, passing Widewell Plantation on your right, until you come to a junction with the A379. With care here, cross over to a minor road opposite, proceeding half right, which takes you past the church and into Stokenham.

D Stokenham

The village has a large and beautifully positioned church. The excellent tower was built in the early 17th century. Inside there is some good Victorian stained glass and a fine pulpit from the same period.

d Walk past the church and Church House Inn, then turn right just before the Tradesmen's Arms Inn. Walk uphill to Kiln Lane, turn right, and then left by Kiln Lodge, following the road uphill for about 250 yards (228m) to reach a footpath on the left (807432). Take this, following it across three fields to reach a road junction at Coleridge Cross. Turn right, following a minor road for Slapton. The road goes gently downhill, then more steeply down as it approaches Deer Bridge. Cross the bridge and, after about 30 yards (27m), turn right, seawards, along a reed-and tree-fringed path. At a path junction, bear left (N) for a short, but worthwhile, detour into Slapton village.

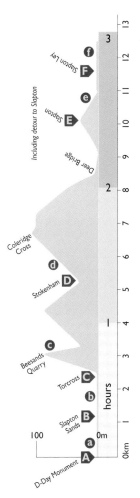

Please note: time taken calculated according to the Naismith Formula (see p.2)

E Slapton

The ruined tower at the northern end of the village is all that remains of a College of Chantry, a small monastic house set up in the 14th century by Sir Guy de Brien. One-time steward to Edward III, Sir Guy built the college and provided for four chaplains who, on a rota, celebrated a daily service and an annual mass for the benefit of the souls of Sir Guy and his family. The celebrations were to last in perpetuity but, just as with the larger monastic houses, the college was dissolved by Henry VIII. Sir Guy is not buried here but in Tewkesbury Abbey in Gloucestershire.

Close to the tower is the village inn which is said to incorporate the cottages in which the masons building the tower lived. To the south of the tower is the village church, a fine 14th century building. In the porch is a medieval sanctuary ring: felons grasping the ring before they were apprehended were granted the right of sanctuary.

Before the D-Day rehearsals Slapton extended along the road towards the A379, that area being known as Slapton Cellars as it had begun, in the 16th century, as a group of fishermen's storage buildings. Later, an inn – the Sands Hotel, but becoming the Royal Sands Hotel after the Prince of Wales (later Edward VII) stayed briefly – and some houses were added. Unfortunately, during the military occupation Pincher, a village dog came back, looking out a few favourite places. He triggered a land mine and the bang set off a series of explosions which destroyed that section of the village. History does not record Pincher's fate, but it can be reasonably assumed that the explosions destroyed him too. The starting car park occupies the site on which the Royal Sands Hotel stood.

The Chantry Tower, Slapton village

e Back on the route (819444), the walk continues south-eastwards along a board walk. Keep to the right at the end of the board walk, towards Slapton Ley and seawards.

F Slapton Ley

The freshwater lagoon, which is divided into two by the causeway which carries the road into Slapton from the A379, is a National Nature Reserve, set up to protect its plantlife, and its breeding and migratory birds. The reed beds are home to Savi's and Cetti's warblers and great crested grebes while migratory species include Slavonian and red-necked grebes, divers and geese. Rare visitors have included purple herons, little bitterns and firecrests. There is a Field Studies Centre at the entrance to Slapton village which administers the SSSI. Slapton Ley is the largest lake in Devon, but is quite shallow, the Lower Ley, the deepest part, being only 6ft (2m) on average.

f   Our route beside the Ley passes an area where elm trees are regenerating by suckering from trees killed by Dutch Elm disease. There are also alder and willow here, the bird life including long-tailed tits and kingfishers. Further on the board walk crosses a boggier section of the Ley: look out for iris, water mint and loosestrife here. A stile on the left gives access to another marshy section of the Ley and a pond which is popular with coots, ducks and geese.

The route continues beside the Ley: there is open water to the right now, and a blockhouse – a reminder of the D-Day preparations – is soon passed. Beyond is an old lime kiln now used by a Reserve warden. When the road is reached a left turn offers a short detour to a bank (on the right) that is a favourite haunt of adders. The route turns right along the road, crossing the bridge which divides the Ley to regain the main road. Cross, with care, to return to the start.

Slapton's Lower Ley from near Torcross

BOLT HEAD AND BOLT TAIL

MAPS:
OS Landranger Sheet 202,
Outdoor Leisure Sheet 20

START/FINISH:
At the North Sands car park
(730382), at the southern end
of Salcombe. There is a small
National Trust car park at
Overbecks. The twisting road to
Overbecks from near South
Sands is also used as a linear
car park during the summer
though this can restrict traffic
movement so do be
considerate

DevonBuses X64 and 92;
Western National bus 93 all
stop at Salcombe

DISTANCE/ASCENT:
15 miles (24km)/1,300ft (400m)

APPROXIMATE TIME:
5–6 hours

HIGHEST POINT:
430ft (130m) near Fir Wood
and Higher Soar

REFRESHMENTS:
Available at Overbecks, Hope
Cove and Salcombe

ADVICE:
Long, but straightforward, and
the 6 mile (9.5km) coastal
section is over all too soon. The
walk can, of course, be
completed in either direction,
but is described with the
coastal section as the second
half

O ur third walk in South Devon follows one of the finest stretches of coastline in the country. The start is close to an historic house and fine garden, with a fine cove at half-distance.

A Salcombe
A mid-19th century guide to Devon noted that Salcombe had two inns, but that both were of 'very humble description' and that the local area was 'almost as unknown as Kamchatka'. Leaving aside the extremely curious place of comparison, how does the description match up to today's town? It seems half correct, for though Salcombe is almost as well known as any other beauty spot in Devon – and much better known than most others by the sailing community – it has managed to retain a simple charm.

The town has a castle built by Henry VIII as one in a series to defend the coast against attack from Europe. During the Civil War the castle (which stands at North Sands) was the last in England to remain loyal to the king. It had been repaired at the expense of Sir Edmund Fortescue, who renamed it Fort Charles in the king's honour . Sir Edmund also recruited and paid the wages of a garrison of troops. These troops – 66 in total, but accompanied by 2 washer women – defied a Parliamentarian army under Fairfax from January 1646 until 3 June when Fortescue finally surrendered. Fairfax bombarded the castle with cannon from Portlemouth Downs, across the estuary, the Parliamentarian gun pits still being visible there. So impressed were the Parliamentarians with the Royalist defiance that Fortescue was allowed to march his men out of the castle with their colours flying.

The well-sheltered estuary on which the town is set, with its numerous inlets, was a centre for the building of schooners in the 19th century, the Salcombe ships achieving fame for their speed across the Atlantic: Salcombe was almost always the first town to off-load this year's pineapples and oranges. The town's history, especially its maritime history, is explored in the museum below the Tourist Information Office in Market Street.

a From the North Sands car park follow the road past South Sands, then uphill to reach the main entrance of the National

Trust's Overbecks Estate. This is the most unforgiving part of the walk and it is very easy to see why the road has so many cars parked along its length.

B Overbecks

The fine Edwardian house was the home, from 1928–37 of Otto Overbeck a scientist. It is named for him and contains his eclectic collections of dolls and toys; equipment and tools from the local shipbuilding trade; a polyphon (a 19th century 'jukebox'); shells, stuffed birds and animals and other items on natural history; and much more. Part of the house is a Youth Hostel.

The gardens surrounding the house are as appealing as the house. The sheltered Salcombe estuary enjoys a very equitable climate and to the surprise of many visitors palm trees and other sub-tropical species thrive. The terraced

Salcombe from the garden at Overbecks

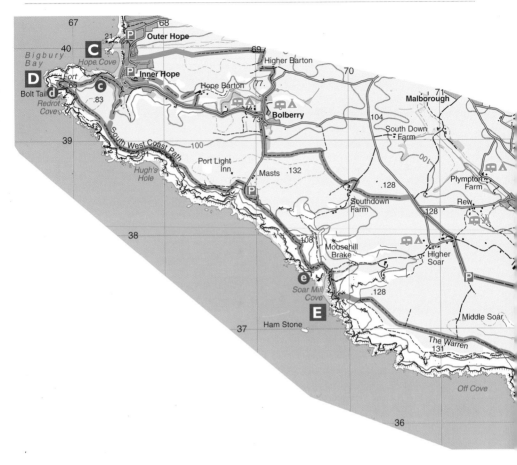

gardens were first laid out in 1901 by an earlier owner, but were enlarged and maintained by subsequent owners, including Overbecks. The gardens have many exotic and rare species of shrubs and trees, many of them tropical. From the path beyond the lawn which fronts the house there is a magnificent view of Salcombe Harbour, framed by palm trees.

b At the entrance to the gardens, bear right along a clear path, following it to, and up, a flight of steps to reach the cliff-top path. Follow the path past the forlorn 426ft (130m) trig. point (728371). Continue round to where the cliff path is above Sharp Tor (728367), for superb views across the estuary to Prawle Point. The path now turns right, to follow the cliffs above Starehole Bottom and heads inland, to intersect a cross path, where the way continues ahead (W then N), through East Soar Farm, then north and west to a

lane with a small car park. Turn right (N) along the lane, passing an old coastguard station at a road junction. Maintain direction (NW) along the road, passing an intersecting road just before the next junction. Here (at 708383) take the field path left (W) through Southdown Farm, then north-west to a bridleway enclosed by hedges (697389); turn left along this bridleway to meet a minor road, then right (N), and left along a short length of often busy road (between Bolberry Cross and Hope Cove) to its next left turn – an option at quiet times for ½ mile (800m), reaching a NT path (stile right) at Hope Barton. Continue northward here through Bolberry, then fork left for North Bolberry, where a lane (left) heads west to Higher Barton (691398), bearing round right to reach a field path. Turn left (W) to emerge on the road at Inner Hope, turning left and down through Hope Cove.

C Hope Cove

Something of the old air of a Devon fishing port can still be detected in the two villages of Hope Cove, despite the fact that tourism is now the dominant industry. There are narrow alleys in Outer Hope, the upper village, while Inner Hope has a cluster of old cottages, little changed for centuries, a group of coastguard cottages and a slipway. The villages were set at one of the safest anchorages in this part of Devon, though to reach the cove in a storm ships had to avoid the dangerous cliffs between Bolt Tail and Bolt Head and also avoid the pinnacles of red rock. It is said that the Spanish Armada was first spotted from the cliffs around Beacon Point to the north of Outer Hope.

c The walk continues from the road elbow (675397) just south of the shore, but a few metres round the bend is a short cut to the coastal path (right at 676396). Otherwise, follow the acorn signs of the South West Coast Path westward from the corner, up the steps by the old lifeboat station. The path goes through woodland, then reaches open downland with fine views across the cove and westwards along the coast. Continue along the obvious path to reach Bolt Tail.

Please note: time taken calculated according to the Naismith Formula (see p.2)

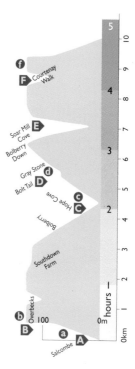

Looking east along the coast at
Bolberry Down

D Bolt Tail

The headland is occupied by a promontory fort constructed in the Iron Age. To defend the headland a ditch was cut across the inland side of a triangle, the other two sides being naturally defended by the cliffs. The Tail is home to shags and cormorants, and sea thrift and wild thyme thrive, but it also has a darker side. Bolt Tail was a landmark feared by sailors in the days before steam power offered some chance of progress against the wind and sea. Ships seeking shelter from a storm in Bigbury Bay could, if their course was too far south, be driven on to the Tail as they tried to turn the headland.

Here in 1760 HMS *Ramilles*, a 90-gun warship carrying troops was driven on to the rocks by a violent storm. The ship's mast snapped and her two anchors dragged. Over 700 men drowned, though 26 actually survived by jumping on to the rocks and escaping being pulled back into the sea by the angry waves and undertow.

d Almost the entire coast from Bolt Tail to Salcombe is owned by the National Trust, its wild beauty preserved for walkers on the coast path as access to cliffs between Bolt Tail and Bolt Head is limited to the two end points – Hope Cove and Salcombe – and to the road end near Bolberry Down. Inland from this section of the cliffs the fields are still home to skylarks, despite the tragic decline in the species numbers.

After enjoying the view north across Bigbury Bay, continue along the coastal path which is both obvious and well waymarked. After crossing Bolberry Down – the road end car park is two fields inland – the path reaches Cathole Cliff, and divides, before dropping steeply into Soar Mill Cove (697376); the path on the left being easier, while the path on the seaward side is steeper but more scenic.

E Soar Mill Cove

Off shore is Ham Stone on which, in 1936, a four-masted Finnish barque, the *Herzogin Cecilie*, was smashed by an April storm. The storm pushed the ship off the rock and into Soar Mill Cove, all the crew being rescued safely. When the weather calmed an attempt was made to tow the ship to Salcombe, but after rounding Bolt Head a sudden squall pushed it aground in Starehole Bay. Before any further salvage attempt could be mounted the weather smashed the ship to pieces, adding her name to the dozens lost on this section of coast. It is said that before the ship's last voyage (from Australia, laden with wheat) her captain woke from a nightmare screaming 'She's on the rocks!'. The ship's owners were unimpressed by this premonition and the ship sailed on time.

e   From the cove the path climbs steeply on to the cliffs of The Warren, where customs men used a tower to watch for smugglers. The foxgloves and gorse are beautiful here.

Follow the path to Bolt Head, from where there is a fine view of the Mew Stones and Starehole Bay. Beyond, the path descends into Starehole Bottom before following the Courtenay Walk, below the cliffs on the outward route.

F   Courtenay Walk

The Walk was cut through the rock and woodland of Sharp Tor in the 19th century by Viscount Courtenay, a son of the Earl of Devon, who wanted easier access to Bolt Head. It now gives one of the most impressive sections of the coast path. As well as local views of the tor edge and woods there are fine views across The Bar to Portlemouth Down and of Salcombe Harbour. The Bar is believed to have been the inspiration for Tennyson's poem *Crossing the Bar*.

f   At the end of the Courtenay Walk the coast path rejoins the outward walk, close to Overbecks: reverse the outward journey to return to the start.

Bolt Head and Starehole Bay from the route near Sharp Tor

COLLINS *rambler's guides*

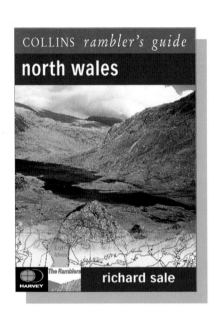

COLLINS *rambler's guide*

north wales

richard sale

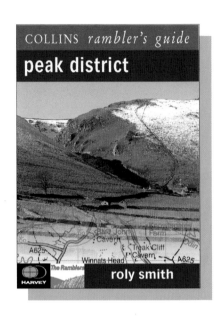

COLLINS *rambler's guide*

peak district

roly smith

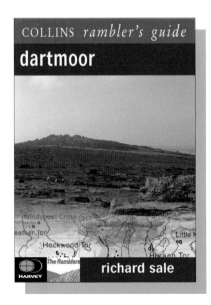

COLLINS *rambler's guide*

dartmoor

richard sale

COLLINS *rambler's guide*

ben nevis & glen coe

chris townsend